Lecture Notes in Computer Science 16399

Founding Editors

Gerhard Goos
Juris Hartmanis

Editorial Board Members

Elisa Bertino, *Purdue University, West Lafayette, IN, USA*
Wen Gao, *Peking University, Beijing, China*
Bernhard Steffen, *TU Dortmund University, Dortmund, Germany*
Moti Yung, *Columbia University, New York, NY, USA*

The series Lecture Notes in Computer Science (LNCS), including its subseries Lecture Notes in Artificial Intelligence (LNAI) and Lecture Notes in Bioinformatics (LNBI), has established itself as a medium for the publication of new developments in computer science and information technology research, teaching, and education.

LNCS enjoys close cooperation with the computer science R & D community, the series counts many renowned academics among its volume editors and paper authors, and collaborates with prestigious societies. Its mission is to serve this international community by providing an invaluable service, mainly focused on the publication of conference and workshop proceedings and postproceedings. LNCS commenced publication in 1973.

Muhammad Imran · Jonathan R. Krebs ·
Michol A. Cooper · Jun Ma · Yuyin Zhou ·
Wei Shao

Editors

Multi-class Segmentation of the Aorta

AortaSeg 2024 Challenge
Held in Conjunction with MICCAI 2024
Virtual Event, October 24, 2024
Proceedings

Editors
Muhammad Imran
Kennesaw State University
Kennesaw, GA, USA

Michol A. Cooper
University of Florida
Gainesville, FL, USA

Yuyin Zhou
University of California
Santa Cruz, CA, USA

Jonathan R. Krebs
University of Florida
Gainesville, FL, USA

Jun Ma
University Health Network
Toronto, ON, Canada

Wei Shao
University of Florida
Gainesville, FL, USA

ISSN 0302-9743　　　　　　　ISSN 1611-3349 (electronic)
Lecture Notes in Computer Science
ISBN 978-3-032-14245-0　　　　ISBN 978-3-032-14246-7 (eBook)
https://doi.org/10.1007/978-3-032-14246-7

This Springer imprint is published by the registered company Springer Nature Switzerland AG
The registered company address is: Gewerbestrasse 11, 6330 Cham, Switzerland

If disposing of this product, please recycle the paper.

Preface

The AortaSeg24 Challenge was organized as part of the 2024 International Conference on Medical Image Computing and Computer Assisted Intervention (MICCAI). Held virtually and hosted by the University of Florida, this challenge aimed to advance the field of medical image segmentation by introducing the first large-scale, publicly available dataset for multi-class segmentation of the aorta, its branches, and clinically relevant zones in computed tomography angiography (CTA).

Aortic dissection is a life-threatening condition that requires precise anatomical understanding for effective diagnosis and treatment. Existing segmentation methods often simplify the problem to binary classification, overlooking the anatomical complexity and clinical importance of differentiating aortic zones and branches. To address this gap, the AortaSeg24 Challenge introduced a dataset of 100 CTA volumes annotated for 23 distinct aortic branches and SVS/STS zones. This dataset was designed to support the development of robust, clinically useful segmentation algorithms.

The challenge attracted over 300 applications, with 121 teams approved to participate. Following a rigorous three-phase process (development, validation, and testing), 16 finalist teams submitted Docker containers for evaluation on 40 hidden test cases. The evaluation was based on two metrics: Dice Similarity Coefficient (DSC) and Normalized Surface Distance (NSD), ensuring a comprehensive assessment of both shape overlap and boundary alignment.

The peer review process was single-blind, with each submission receiving an average of two reviews. External reviewers were involved to ensure objectivity, and the Open-Review platform was used for submission and evaluation. Only the 16 top-performing teams among more than 100 participants were invited to submit papers. We received 10 submissions, all of which were accepted as full papers after a thorough review process.

The top five teams were awarded cash prizes, and the top ten received honorable mention certificates. Teams that made their code publicly available and surpassed the baseline model were invited to co-author the challenge review paper. This collaborative effort reflects the challenge's commitment to transparency, reproducibility, and scientific rigor.

We hope that the resources and insights generated through AortaSeg24 will foster continued innovation in vascular imaging and support improved clinical outcomes for patients with aortic disease.

November 2025
Muhammad Imran
Jonathan R. Krebs
Michol A. Cooper
Jun Ma
Yuyin Zhou
Wei Shao

Organization

General Chair

Wei Shao University of Florida, USA

Program Committee Chairs

Muhammad Imran Kennesaw State University, USA
Jonathan R. Krebs University of Florida, USA
Michol A. Cooper University of Florida, USA
Jun Ma University Health Network, Canada
Yuyin Zhou University of California, Santa Cruz, USA
Wei Shao (Contact Editor) University of Florida, USA

Steering Committee

Muhammad Imran Kennesaw State University, USA
Jonathan R. Krebs University of Florida, USA
Michol A. Cooper University of Florida, USA
Jun Ma University Health Network, Canada
Yuyin Zhou University of California, Santa Cruz, USA
Wei Shao University of Florida, USA

Program Committee Members

Bong Thanh Nguyen MedAI/Korea University, South Korea
Bo Liu Beihang University, China
Henning Müller University of Applied Sciences Western Switzerland (HES-SO), Switzerland
Jinghua Yue Beihang University, China
Kaixiang Yang Wuhan National Laboratory for Optoelectronics, Huazhong University of Science and Technology, China
Kwang-Hyun Uhm MedAI/Korea University, South Korea
Muhammad Imran Kennesaw State University, USA

Marek Wodzinski	AGH University of Krakow, Poland
Markus Tiefenthaler	Medical University of Innsbruck, Austria
Moona Mazher	University College London, UK
Pengcheng Shi	Harbin Institute of Technology (Shenzhen), China
Steven A. Niederer	Imperial College London, UK

Contents

Multi-Class Segmentation of Aortic Branches and Zones in CTA

Coarse-to-Fine Aortic Segmentation on CTA Using a Two-Stage nnUNet-Based Framework

Jinlong Huang, Xiao Sun, and Lisheng Wang

Institute of Image Processing and Pattern Recognition, Shanghai Jiao Tong University, Shanghai 200240, China
lswang@sjtu.edu.cn

Abstract. Precise, automated segmentation of the aorta and its branches from Computed Tomography Angiography (CTA) is crucial for preoperative planning of endovascular treatments. However, this task is challenging due to the complex topology, significant anatomical variation, and the fine-scale nature of smaller vessels. This paper presents a coarse-to-fine, two-stage segmentation framework built upon the robust nnUNet architecture to address these challenges. In the first stage, a coarse segmentation is performed on downsampled images to efficiently localize a region of interest (ROI) containing the entire aorta. The second stage employs a fine-grained segmentation network on the full-resolution cropped ROI, enabling detailed and accurate delineation of aortic branches and zones. Our method utilizes an ensemble of nnUNet models with residual encoder backbones (ResEncL and ResEncM) to enhance feature extraction and improve generalization. The final segmentation is produced by a weighted average of predictions from multiple models. On the AortaSeg24 challenge testing dataset, our method achieves a competitive mean Dice Similarity Coefficient (DSC) of 0.782 and a mean Normalized Surface Distance (NSD) of 0.817, demonstrating the effectiveness of the two-stage approach for complex vascular segmentation. The source code is publicly available at https://github.com/MaxwellEng/MICCAI_CHANLLENGE24_HJL.

Keywords: Aorta Segmentation · Computed Tomography · Complicated ROIs

1 Introduction

1.1 Background

The aorta is the body's largest artery, supplying oxygenated blood to all major organ systems. Pathologies such as dissection, aneurysm, and atherosclerotic disease affecting the aorta and its branches can be life-threatening and require prompt intervention [3]. Recent advancements in endovascular grafting have

© The Author(s), under exclusive license to Springer Nature Switzerland AG 2026
M. Imran et al. (Eds.): AortaSeg 2024, LNCS 16399, pp. 3–11, 2026.
https://doi.org/10.1007/978-3-032-14246-7_1

introduced minimally invasive treatment options, for which precise preoperative planning is paramount. Accurate 3D multi-class segmentation of the aorta and its branch vessels from CTA scans is essential for creating patient-specific surgical plans and designing custom endografts, as illustrated in Fig. 1. Manual segmentation is time-consuming, tedious, and subject to inter-observer variability. Therefore, developing an accurate and automated segmentation method is a critical need in clinical practice to improve efficiency and standardization. This work addresses the AortaSeg24 challenge [2], which aims to benchmark automated methods for this task.

Fig. 1. 3D visualization of the multi-class aorta segmentation, highlighting the complex branching structure addressed in this work.

1.2 Related Work

The nnUNet framework [1] has become the de facto standard in medical image segmentation, consistently achieving state-of-the-art performance by automatically configuring its pipeline for new datasets. Our work adopts nnUNet, specifically its recently proposed residual encoder variants [5], as a strong foundation.

A key challenge in vascular segmentation is maintaining the connectivity of thin, elongated structures. Standard overlap-based losses like Dice can fail in these scenarios. To mitigate this, topology-aware losses have been developed. For instance, Skeleton Recall Loss [4] was designed to enforce vessel connectivity efficiently without high computational overhead, making it suitable for multi-class segmentation.

For complex aortic anatomies, specialized architectures have also been explored. CIS-UNet [6] integrated a transformer-based attention mechanism into a U-Net to capture global context, demonstrating improved performance over standard baselines for multi-class aorta segmentation. These works underscore the importance of robust backbones, appropriate loss functions, and context-aware architectures for this challenging task.

1.3   Contributions

The main contributions of this work are:

1. We propose a two-stage, coarse-to-fine segmentation pipeline that first localizes the aorta at low resolution and then performs high-resolution segmentation on a focused ROI, balancing computational efficiency and accuracy.
2. We leverage nnUNet with powerful residual encoder backbones (ResEncM and ResEncL) and an ensemble strategy that combines predictions from multiple models to achieve robust and generalizable performance.
3. We demonstrate the effectiveness of our framework on the AortaSeg24 challenge, achieving a competitive mean Dice score of 0.782 on the final test set.

2   Method

Our methodology is a two-stage coarse-to-fine framework designed to efficiently and accurately segment the aorta and its complex branch structures from CTA images. The overall pipeline is illustrated in Fig. 2.

2.1   Network Architecture

The core of our method is a two-stage approach:

Stage 1: Coarse ROI Localization. The full-resolution CTA images are large, making direct processing computationally expensive. To address this, we first train an nnUNet model ('*3d_lowres*' configuration) on images downsampled to an isotropic spacing of $1.9\,\mathrm{mm}^3$. This coarse model rapidly generates a low-resolution binary mask of the entire aorta. A bounding box is then extracted from this mask, defining a region of interest (ROI) that robustly encapsulates the entire aortic structure.

Stage 2: Fine-Grained Segmentation. The ROI identified in the first stage is used to crop the original, full-resolution image. A second set of nnUNet models is trained exclusively on these high-resolution cropped patches. This allows the network to focus its capacity on learning the fine details of the aortic branches and zones without being burdened by irrelevant background information. We use two powerful residual encoder variants for this stage: ResEncM and ResEncL, which feature deeper architectures than the standard nnUNet '*3d_fullres*' configuration (see Table 1).

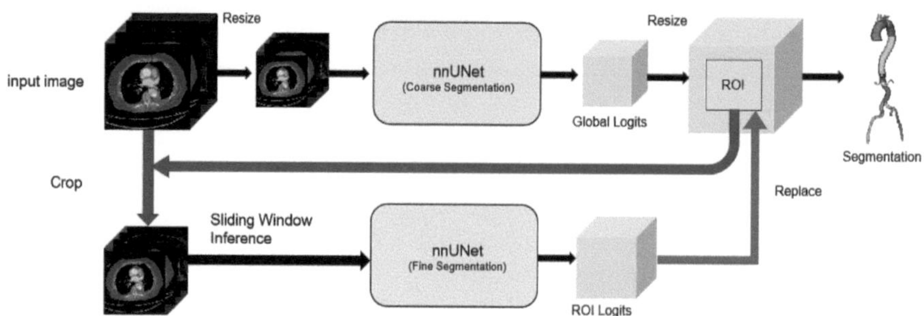

Fig. 2. Overview of our two-stage coarse-to-fine segmentation framework. (**1**) In the coarse stage, a '3*d_lowres*' nnUNet processes the downsampled full image to predict a low-resolution mask. (**2**) A bounding box (ROI) is extracted from this mask. (**3**) In the fine stage, the ROI is used to crop the original full-resolution image. (**4**) An ensemble of fine-grained nnUNet models (with ResEncM/L backbones) segments the cropped high-resolution volume. (**5**) The final multi-class segmentation is generated.

2.2   Pre-processing

All CTA volumes are first resampled to an isotropic spacing of $1.0\,\mathrm{mm}^3$ using third-order spline interpolation. Image intensities are then normalized by clipping to the [0.5, 99.5] percentile range of non-zero voxels and scaling to a range of [0, 1] with zero mean and unit variance. This standardization step ensures consistent input for the network.

2.3   Loss Function

The models in both stages are trained using a combination of Dice loss and Cross-Entropy (CE) loss. This hybrid loss function is a standard and effective choice in medical image segmentation, balancing performance on both global structure and voxel-level classification. The total loss $\mathcal{L}_{\text{total}}$ is defined as:

$$\mathcal{L}_{\text{total}}(\boldsymbol{\theta}) = \mathcal{L}_{\text{Dice}}(\boldsymbol{\theta}) + \mathcal{L}_{\text{CE}}(\boldsymbol{\theta}) \tag{1}$$

where $\mathcal{L}_{\text{Dice}}$ is the multi-class Dice loss and $\mathcal{L}_{\text{CE}}$ is the multi-class Cross-Entropy loss. We initially experimented with topology-aware losses like Skeleton Recall Loss [4] but observed no significant performance improvement on the validation set for this specific dataset, likely due to the sufficient resolution of the vessel structures. Therefore, we proceeded with the Dice and CE combination.

2.4   Post-processing and Ensembling

To further boost performance and robustness, we employ an ensemble strategy in the fine-grained stage. Our final prediction is a weighted average of the outputs from five different models: three trained with the ResEncM architecture and two with the ResEncL architecture. No further complex post-processing steps, such as removing small connected components, were applied, as the ensembled model predictions were generally clean.

3 Experiments

3.1 Dataset and Evaluation Metrics

We trained and evaluated our method on the AortaSeg24 challenge dataset, which contains 100 abdominal CTA scans with multi-class annotations for the aorta, its primary branches, and clinically relevant zones. For our internal development, the official training set of 50 images was split into a 40-image training set and a 10-image validation set (80/20 split). The final evaluation was performed on the official hidden test set of 40 images. The primary evaluation metrics are the Dice Similarity Coefficient (DSC) and the Normalized Surface Distance (NSD).

3.2 Implementation Details

Our framework was implemented using PyTorch. All models were trained for 1000 epochs using the Adam optimizer with an initial learning rate of 0.01 and a poly learning rate decay schedule. Standard nnUNet data augmentation techniques were applied, including random rotations, scaling, and elastic deformations. Details of the network architectures are provided in Table 1. The training environment and protocol are summarized in Tables 2 and 3.

Table 1. Architecture configurations for the coarse and fine stages, including features per stage and input patch size.

Architecture	Features per Stage	Patch Size
3d_lowres (Coarse)	32, 64, 128, 256, 320	$112 \times 192 \times 192$
ResEncM (Fine)	32, 64, 128, 256, 320	$160 \times 160 \times 256$
ResEncL (Fine)	32, 64, 128, 256, 320, 320	$160 \times 160 \times 256$

4 Results and Discussion

4.1 Performance Evaluation

We evaluated our framework through the official AortaSeg24 challenge platform. The performance on the online validation set, summarized in Table 4, demonstrates the effectiveness of our approach, achieving a mean Dice score of 0.762. This strong performance secured a top rank during the validation phase of the challenge. The per-class scores highlight that while larger structures were segmented accurately, challenges remained in delineating smaller, more variable vessels like the Left Renal Artery (DSC 0.587), indicating areas for potential improvement.

The final quantitative results on the hidden test set of 40 cases are presented in Table 5. As shown in Table 5, our proposed method consistently outperforms

Table 2. Training environment details (mandatory table).

Component	Specification
Hardware	Single NVIDIA GeForce RTX 3090 GPU
GPU Memory	24 GB
CPU	Intel Core i9-12900K
RAM	64 GB
Operating System	Ubuntu 20.04
Software	Python 3.9, PyTorch 1.12, CUDA 11.6

Table 3. Training protocol details (mandatory table).

Parameter	Value
Optimizer	Adam
Learning Rate	Initial: 10^{-2}, Schedule: PolyLR
Loss Function	Dice + Cross-Entropy
Batch Size	2
Patch Size	See Table 1
Epochs	1000
Data Augmentation	Rotation, Scaling, Elastic Deformation, Gamma Correction

Table 4. Performance of our method on the AortaSeg24 online validation set. DSC scores are reported for each anatomical class.

Aortic branch	DSC	Aortic branch	DSC
SMA	0.702	Celiac Artery	0.714
Zone 0	0.879	Left Renal Artery	0.587
Zone 1	0.658	Right Renal Artery	0.672
Zone 2	0.741	Left Common Carotid	0.745
Zone 3	0.791	Left Subclavian Artery	0.793
Zone 4	0.805	Left Internal Iliac Artery	0.692
Zone 5	0.884	Right Internal Iliac Artery	0.764
Zone 6	0.695	Zone 10 L	0.829
Zone 7	0.695	Zone 10 R	0.835
Zone 8	0.757	Zone 11 L	0.790
Zone 9	0.891	Zone 11 R	0.820
Innominate	0.793	**Average**	**0.762**

the baseline CIS-UNet [6] across most anatomical regions of the AortaSeg24 testing dataset. In particular, our model achieves an overall Dice score of 0.782

Table 5. Quantitative evaluation on the AortaSeg24 testing dataset. The table reports average Dice and NSD scores (mean ± standard deviation) across all 40 test cases for each anatomical region. Authors may expand this table to include ablation studies or additional baselines. (mandatory table)

Anatomical Region	Our Method		Baseline Method [6]	
	Avg. DSC	Avg. NSD	Avg. DSC	Avg. NSD
Zone 0	0.898 ± 0.053	0.808 ± 0.114	0.880 ± 0.064	0.773 ± 0.119
Innominate	0.784 ± 0.121	0.840 ± 0.134	0.691 ± 0.164	0.739 ± 0.175
Zone 1	0.646 ± 0.157	0.582 ± 0.157	0.604 ± 0.164	0.560 ± 0.150
Left Common Carotid	0.815 ± 0.052	0.931 ± 0.048	0.743 ± 0.108	0.837 ± 0.117
Zone 2	0.713 ± 0.112	0.598 ± 0.148	0.659 ± 0.143	0.543 ± 0.153
Left Subclavian Artery	0.827 ± 0.076	0.908 ± 0.095	0.789 ± 0.115	0.859 ± 0.115
Zone 3	0.720 ± 0.137	0.593 ± 0.151	0.660 ± 0.171	0.517 ± 0.181
Zone 4	0.796 ± 0.100	0.687 ± 0.123	0.746 ± 0.122	0.620 ± 0.139
Zone 5	0.910 ± 0.035	0.876 ± 0.065	0.879 ± 0.054	0.826 ± 0.096
Zone 6	0.716 ± 0.111	0.654 ± 0.154	0.731 ± 0.123	0.678 ± 0.164
Celiac Artery	0.655 ± 0.167	0.835 ± 0.159	0.568 ± 0.178	0.728 ± 0.168
Zone 7	0.715 ± 0.126	0.685 ± 0.149	0.699 ± 0.116	0.660 ± 0.146
SMA	0.753 ± 0.091	0.871 ± 0.098	0.678 ± 0.131	0.782 ± 0.135
Zone 8	0.701 ± 0.122	0.691 ± 0.137	0.664 ± 0.160	0.656 ± 0.160
Right Renal Artery	0.729 ± 0.133	0.892 ± 0.144	0.697 ± 0.142	0.851 ± 0.140
Left Renal Artery	0.680 ± 0.165	0.834 ± 0.160	0.593 ± 0.199	0.742 ± 0.216
Zone 9	0.919 ± 0.030	0.918 ± 0.075	0.879 ± 0.081	0.860 ± 0.130
Right Common Iliac Artery	0.867 ± 0.059	0.918 ± 0.079	0.800 ± 0.132	0.840 ± 0.148
Left Common Iliac Artery	0.871 ± 0.035	0.935 ± 0.061	0.786 ± 0.135	0.842 ± 0.164
Right Internal Iliac Artery	0.791 ± 0.070	0.922 ± 0.075	0.661 ± 0.167	0.773 ± 0.179
Left Internal Iliac Artery	0.748 ± 0.126	0.880 ± 0.113	0.640 ± 0.197	0.767 ± 0.205
Right External Iliac Artery	0.875 ± 0.057	0.966 ± 0.050	0.789 ± 0.134	0.846 ± 0.143
Left External Iliac Artery	0.869 ± 0.049	0.957 ± 0.048	0.783 ± 0.151	0.851 ± 0.160
Overall	**0.782 ± 0.025**	**0.817 ± 0.027**	**0.723 ± 0.058**	**0.746 ± 0.067**

± 0.025 and an overall NSD of 0.817 ± 0.027, surpassing the baseline results of 0.723 ± 0.058 and 0.746 ± 0.067, respectively. The improvements are especially notable in smaller and more complex vascular branches such as the left common carotid and iliac arteries, indicating the model's enhanced ability to capture fine-grained anatomical details and maintain spatial continuity along the aortic tree. These results demonstrate that our method achieves more accurate and robust segmentation performance, reflecting better generalization to test cases.

Our proposed two-stage, coarse-to-fine framework demonstrates strong performance on the AortaSeg24 challenge. The initial coarse localization step effectively reduces the computational burden and allows the subsequent fine-grained models to focus on the anatomically complex ROI at full resolution. This strategy is particularly well-suited for large-volume scans like CTA. The use of an ensemble of models with powerful ResEnc backbones further contributes to the robustness of the final segmentation, averaging out minor errors from individual models.

The quantitative results in Table 5 align with expectations for this task: larger, more consistent structures (e.g., aortic zones in the descending aorta) achieve higher DSC scores, while smaller, more anatomically variable arteries (e.g., renal and celiac arteries) are more challenging to segment accurately. This suggests that future work could focus on methods specifically designed to improve the segmentation of these fine-scale vessels.

One limitation of our current work is the lack of extensive ablation studies to isolate the contribution of each component (e.g., coarse-to-fine strategy vs. a single-stage approach, or the impact of each ResEnc variant). The ensemble weights were also determined empirically, and a more systematic optimization could potentially yield further improvements.

5   Conclusion

In this study, we presented an effective two-stage nnUNet-based framework for multi-class aortic segmentation. By combining a coarse localization stage with a fine-grained, ensemble-based segmentation stage, our method achieves competitive accuracy on the challenging AortaSeg24 dataset. This automated approach has the potential to provide valuable support in clinical workflows for planning endovascular procedures.

For future work, we plan to conduct detailed ablation studies to quantify the impact of each component of our pipeline. Furthermore, we will explore advanced loss functions, such as topology-aware or boundary-focused losses, to specifically target the challenges of segmenting small and intricate vessel branches. Integrating attention mechanisms, similar to those in CIS-UNet [6], could also enhance the model's ability to capture long-range dependencies and improve overall performance.

Acknowledgments. We thank all data contributors for making the medical images publicly available, and GrandChallenge for providing the challenge platform.

Disclosure of Interests. The authors have no competing interests to declare that are relevant to the content of this article.

Ethical Compliance Statement. All data used was publicly available and anonymized.

References

1. Isensee, F., Jaeger, P.F., Kohl, S.A., Petersen, J., Maier-Hein, K.H.: nnU-Net: a self-configuring method for deep learning-based biomedical image segmentation. Nat. Methods **18**(2), 203–211 (2021)

2. Imran, M., et al.: Multi-Class Segmentation of Aortic Branches and Zones in Computed Tomography Angiography: The AortaSeg24 Challenge. arXiv preprint arXiv:2502.05330 (2025)
3. Krebs, J.R., et al.: Volumetric analysis of acute uncomplicated type B aortic dissection using an automated deep learning aortic zone segmentation model. J. Vasc. Surg. **80**(4), 1025–1034 (2024)
4. Kirchhoff, Y., et al.: Skeleton Recall Loss for Connectivity Conserving and Resource Efficient Segmentation of Thin Tubular Structures. arXiv preprint arXiv:2404.03010 (2024)
5. Isensee, F., et al.: nnU-Net Revisited: A Call for Rigorous Validation in 3D Medical Image Segmentation. arXiv preprint arXiv:2404.09556 (2024)
6. Imran, M., et al.: CIS-UNet: multi-class segmentation of the aorta in computed tomography angiography via context-aware shifted window self-attention. Comput. Med. Imaging Graph **118**, 102470 (2024)
7. Ma, J., et al.: Loss odyssey in medical image segmentation. Med. Image Anal. **71**, 102035 (2021)

Hierarchical Semantic Learning for Multi-class Aorta Segmentation

Pengcheng Shi[1,2]([✉])

[1] Medical Image Insights, Foundation Models Division, Shanghai, China
shipc1220@gmail.com
[2] Harbin Institute of Technology (Shenzhen), Shenzhen, China

Abstract. The aorta, the body's largest artery, is prone to pathologies such as dissection, aneurysm, and atherosclerosis, which often require timely intervention. Minimally invasive repairs involving branch vessels necessitate detailed 3D anatomical analysis. Existing methods often overlook hierarchical anatomical relationships while struggling with severe class imbalance inherent in vascular structures. To address these challenges, we propose a hierarchical semantic learning strategy combined with curriculum learning principles. Inspired by human cognition, our approach progressively learns anatomical constraints by decomposing complex structures from simple to complex components. The curriculum learning framework naturally addresses class imbalance by first establishing robust feature representations for dominant classes before tackling rare but anatomically critical structures, significantly accelerating model convergence in multi-class scenarios. Additionally, we introduce a centerline boundary Dice (cbDice) loss function that incorporates geometric priors to ensure consistent segmentation across varying vessel diameters while mitigating class imbalance effects. Our two-stage inference strategy achieves up to fivefold acceleration, enhancing clinical practicality. On the validation set at epoch 50, our hierarchical semantic loss improves the Dice score of nnU-Net ResEnc M by 11.65%. The proposed model demonstrates a 5.6% higher Dice score than baselines on the test set. Experimental results show significant improvements in segmentation accuracy and efficiency, making the framework suitable for real-time clinical applications.

Keywords: Hierarchical semantics · Curriculum learning · Class imbalance · Vascular segmentation

1 Introduction

Minimally invasive aortic repairs require precise 3D anatomical analysis, which can be achieved through multi-class segmentation of the aorta in CTA to facilitate appropriate device selection. However, current segmentation methods face two fundamental challenges: (1) they often ignore the hierarchical anatomical information of vascular structures, which is essential for preserving anatomical

M. Imran et al. (Eds.): AortaSeg 2024, LNCS 16399, pp. 12–22, 2026.
https://doi.org/10.1007/978-3-032-14246-7_2

consistency, and (2) they struggle with severe class imbalance inherent in vascular networks, where major vessels dominate while critical branch structures appear only sparsely.

The challenge of class imbalance in tubular structure segmentation is particularly pronounced, where the volume ratio between dominant classes and fine peripheral vessels can be extremely large. Conventional approaches like class reweighting or focal loss [10] often fail to fully utilize the natural semantic hierarchy. Instead, our reference to the hierarchical semantic segmentation network (HSSN) [8] addresses this imbalance by incorporating structural curriculum learning, where the model first learns to distinguish merged large-volume classes before progressing to finer branch-level distinctions.

In this paper, we propose a novel hierarchical semantic learning framework for multi-class aorta segmentation that incorporates curriculum learning principles. Curriculum learning, where examples are introduced progressively from simple to complex [1], provides a natural solution to class imbalance by first establishing robust feature representations for dominant structures before tackling rare but anatomically critical branches. This approach mirrors the hierarchical learning process observed in human cognition [12], allowing the model to find a more optimal parameter space while simultaneously addressing the class imbalance problem. The combination of hierarchical semantics with curriculum learning proves particularly effective for vascular segmentation, where the progressive learning strategy significantly accelerates convergence compared to flat learning paradigms, especially when dealing with numerous anatomical classes. Our model decomposes anatomical semantics from simpler to more complex structures, utilizing a hierarchical semantic tree to ensure consistent and anatomically sound segmentation while explicitly modeling the relative prevalence of different vascular classes.

The integration of the cbDice loss function further ensures uniform segmentation across classes while maintaining the vascular network's topological integrity, with the boundary-aware formulation naturally compensating for class imbalance through geometric constraints rather than simple frequency-based reweighting. The two-stage inference method first segments all foreground vessels using a low-resolution 3D model, followed by multi-class segmentation in a refined region of interest (ROI). This hierarchical processing not only reduces inference time by up to 5x but also helps mitigate class imbalance by focusing computational resources on regions containing minority classes.

NexToU extends these concepts by incorporating a hierarchical semantic tree that explicitly models prevalence relationships between classes, allowing the network to leverage the natural anatomical hierarchy when learning rare classes. The hierarchical constraints also serve as a form of data augmentation for minority classes, as correctly predicting their parent classes in the hierarchy provides strong spatial priors for their location. The implementation code for this challenge entry is publicly available at: https://github.com/PengchengShi1220/AortaSeg24.

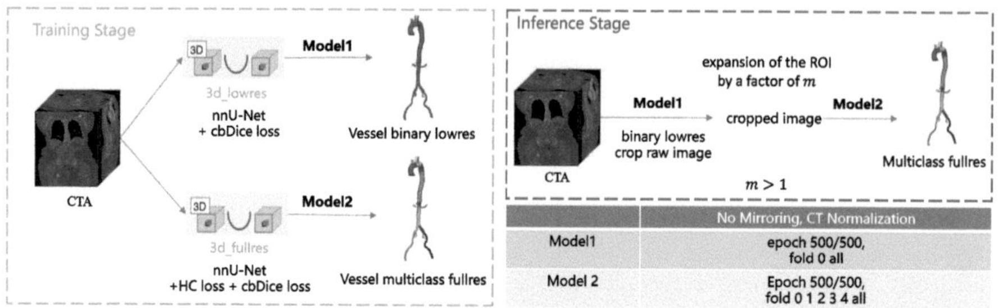

Fig. 1. The two-stage inference approach improves speed by up to 5 times compared to using only Model 2, depending on the expansion factor m of the ROI in the first stage.

1.1 Hierarchical Semantic Learning

Hierarchical semantic learning (HSL) addresses the inherent limitations of conventional pixel-wise segmentation methods by incorporating structured class relationships into the learning process. Unlike flat segmentation approaches that enforce only fine-grained semantic constraints [6], HSL leverages multi-level semantic hierarchies to improve feature discrimination, particularly in homogeneous multi-class tubular structures. This paradigm aligns with human cognition, where understanding progresses from coarse classes to fine-grained classes.

1.2 Curriculum Learning

Curriculum learning (CL) progressively introduce samples of increasing complexity. Inspired by human educational strategies [1], CL trains model on easier subsets (e.g., larger organs or isolated structures) before advancing to finer, harder-to-segment classes (e.g., small vessels or overlapping airways). This staged approach is particularly effective for multi-class datasets [6,13], where early exposure to dominant classes can stabilize feature learning before addressing rare or morphologically complex targets. However, current CL implementations often decouple semantic hierarchy from the curriculum, limiting their ability to exploit structural relationships. Integrating HSL with CL—for instance, by sequencing tasks from coarse-to-fine hierarchies—could further enhance model robustness in heterogeneous anatomical segmentation.

2 Methodology

2.1 Fractal Softmax

Drawing inspiration from the HSSN [8], we focus on the hierarchical interrelationships among classes using a tree structure $\mathcal{T} = (\mathcal{V}, \mathcal{E})$. Each node $v \in \mathcal{V}$ symbolizes a semantic (or anatomical) category, with edges $(u, v) \in \mathcal{E}$ denoting hierarchical relationships, where node v is the superclass of u. Layers of tree

$\mathcal{T}$ are denoted by l (where $l = 1, 2, \ldots, L$), with $\mathcal{V}_l$ representing the set of all foreground categories at level l.

For volumetric segmentation, assuming that the 3D input (volume) $\mathbf{x} \in \mathbb{R}^{C \times H \times W \times D}$ with resolution (H, W, D), C base channels. A segmentation network f_{NET} is devised to extract the finest-level leaf predictions $\mathbf{y}_L = f_{\text{NET}}(\mathbf{x})$, where $\mathbf{y}_L \in \mathbb{R}^{(|\mathcal{V}_L|+1) \times H \times W \times D}$.

In addition to the finest level of leaf predictions, for levels $l \in \{L - 1, L - 2, \ldots, 1\}$, our model predicts semantic categories v_l for each pixel y by recursively computing $y_{v_l} = \max_{u \in \mathcal{C}_{v_l}} y_u$. The predictions at each hierarchical level l are represented as $\mathbf{y}_l$, where each class v_l at level l is expressed by $\mathbf{y}_l[v_l] \in \mathbb{R}^{H \times W \times D}$. The set $\mathcal{C}_{v_l}$ encompasses subclasses of node v_l, and $\mathcal{A}_{v_l}$ its superclasses. We apply softmax to $\mathbf{y}_l$ to obtain probabilistic predictions $\mathbf{p}_l$, The process is shown in Algorithm 1.

Algorithm 1. Fractal softmax prediction

Require: Image $\mathbf{x}$, Tree structure $\mathcal{T} = (\mathcal{V}, \mathcal{E})$
Ensure: Hierarchical semantic predictions from the finest (leaf) to the coarsest (root) level
  1: Compute initial leaf predictions $\mathbf{y}_L = f_{\text{NET}}(\mathbf{x})$
  2: **for** $l = L - 1$ to 1 **do**
  3:     Initialize $\mathbf{y}_l$ as an empty tensor of appropriate dimensions
  4:     **for** each node $v_l \in \mathcal{V}_l$ **do**
  5:        Compute subclass set $\mathcal{C}_{v_l}$
  6:        $\mathbf{y}_l[v_l] \leftarrow \max_{u \in \mathcal{C}_{v_l}} \mathbf{y}_{l+1}[u]$
  7:     **end for**
  8:     $\mathbf{p}_l \leftarrow \text{softmax}(\mathbf{y}_l)$
  9: **end for**
10: **return** $\{\mathbf{p}_l\}_{l=1}^{L}$

In the multi-class scenario, the hierarchical tree $\mathcal{T}$ involves various subclasses and superclasses at different levels, as well as sibling categories at the same level, all of which need to fulfill specific properties and constraints. Some properties have been explored in various hierarchical classification works [2,3,14], though some aspects have received less attention. In the context of the HSSN, the hierarchical tree $\mathcal{T}$ is governed by six essential properties or constraints that influence the behavior of the segmentation model (Definitions 1 to 6).

Definition 1 (Positive $\mathcal{T}$-Property). *If a category is marked positive for a pixel, all its ancestor nodes in $\mathcal{T}$ (i.e., superclasses) are also positive.*

Definition 2 (Negative $\mathcal{T}$-Property). *If a category is marked negative for a pixel, all its descendant nodes in $\mathcal{T}$ (i.e., subclasses) are also negative.*

Definition 3 (Positive $\mathcal{T}$-Constraint). *For a positive marked category v and its ancestor u, it must hold that $p_v \leq p_u$.*

Definition 4 (Negative $\mathcal{T}$-Constraint). *For a negative marked category v and its descendant u, it must hold that $1 - p_v \leq 1 - p_u$.*

Definition 5 (Exclusivity $\mathcal{T}$-Property). *If a category at a certain hierarchical level is marked positive, all its sibling nodes (categories at the same level) in $\mathcal{T}$ should be marked negative.*

Definition 6 (Exclusivity $\mathcal{T}$-Constraint). *For a positive marked category v and its sibling u, it should hold that $p_v \leq 1 - p_u$.*

Unlike the HSSN, which employs sigmoid functions for the hierarchical classification of each category $v \in \mathcal{V}$, our method adopts the softmax function to normalize prediction results $\mathbf{y}_l$ at each hierarchical level l. We introduce this as the "fractal softmax" in this paper. It shares certain similarities with the hierarchical recursive generation process of fractal models [9]. This approach is designed to satisfy both the positive and negative $\mathcal{T}$-properties and constraints, as well as the exclusivity properties and constraints, as outlined in Definitions 1 through 6. Further details will be provided in the upcoming version of the NexToU paper. The code is available at https://github.com/PengchengShi1220/NexToU. Figure 2 illustrates the hierarchical semantic tree for the AortaSeg24 dataset, which includes 23 classes. The tree structure captures the relationships between superclasses and subclasses, facilitating the hierarchical learning process.

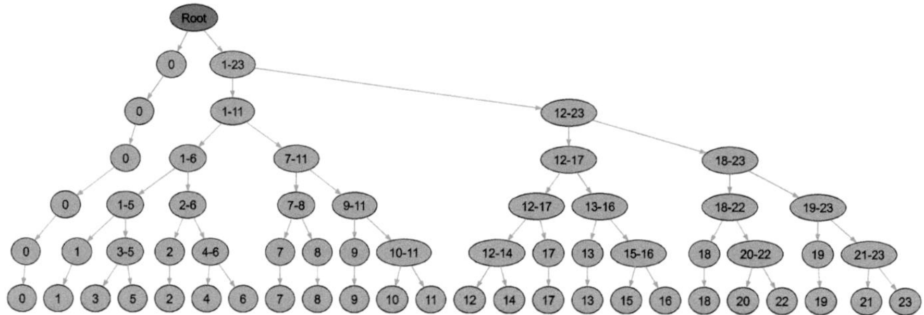

Fig. 2. Hierarchical anatomical tree for AortaSeg24, illustrating superclass-subclass relationships from simple to complex structures.

2.2   Two-Stage Inference

As shown in Fig. 1, the training framework is based on nnU-Net V2 [6]. To enhance efficiency, we adopt a two-stage approach: first, a low-resolution 3D model segments all foreground vessels, followed by multi-class segmentation within an ROI extracted from the original image. This significantly improves inference speed, making the model more suitable for clinical applications.

2.3 Training Details

The cl-X-Dice [11] addresses segmentation challenges for vessels of varying diameters:

$$\mathrm{Tprec}(S_{\mathrm{P}}, S_{\mathrm{L}}, V_{\mathrm{L}}) = \frac{|Q_{\mathrm{sp}} \cap Q_{\mathrm{vl}}|}{|Q_{\mathrm{sp}} \cap Q_{\mathrm{spvp}} \cap (U - S_{\mathrm{L}})| + |Q_{\mathrm{sp}} \cap Q_{\mathrm{slvl}}|} \tag{1}$$

$$\mathrm{Tsens}(S_{\mathrm{L}}, S_{\mathrm{P}}, V_{\mathrm{P}}) = \frac{|Q_{\mathrm{sl}} \cap Q_{\mathrm{vp}}|}{|Q_{\mathrm{sl}} \cap Q_{\mathrm{slvl}} \cap (U - S_{\mathrm{P}})| + |Q_{\mathrm{sl}} \cap Q_{\mathrm{spvp}}|} \tag{2}$$

$$\mathrm{cl\text{-}X\text{-}Dice}(V_{\mathrm{P}}, V_{\mathrm{L}}) = \frac{2 \times \mathrm{Tprec}(S_{\mathrm{P}}, S_{\mathrm{L}}, V_{\mathrm{L}}) \times \mathrm{Tsens}(S_{\mathrm{L}}, S_{\mathrm{P}}, V_{\mathrm{P}})}{\mathrm{Tprec}(S_{\mathrm{P}}, S_{\mathrm{L}}, V_{\mathrm{L}}) + \mathrm{Tsens}(S_{\mathrm{L}}, S_{\mathrm{P}}, V_{\mathrm{P}})} \tag{3}$$

Model training details: - **Model 1:** 500 epochs using low-resolution 3D binary segmentation. - **Model 2:** 1000 epochs for full-resolution multi-class segmentation.

The total loss function combines cross-entropy, Dice, and cBDice. The cross-entropy and Dice components are subjected to L-level constraints:

$$\mathcal{L}(\mathbf{y}, \mathbf{g}) = \frac{1}{\lambda_{\mathrm{sum}}} \sum_{l=1}^{L_s} \lambda_l \cdot (\lambda_{\mathrm{ce}} \cdot \mathcal{L}_{\mathrm{ce}}(\mathbf{y}_l, \mathbf{g}_l) + \lambda_{\mathrm{dice}} \cdot \mathcal{L}_{\mathrm{dice}}(\mathbf{y}_l, \mathbf{g}_l)) + \lambda_{cbDice} \cdot L_{cbDice}$$

$$\tag{4}$$

3 Experiments and Results

3.1 Dataset and Evaluation Protocol

Table 1. Training protocols for the first and second stage models

Training Parameter	Value
Batch size	2
Patch size	$112 \times 112 \times 176$
Total epochs	500
Optimizer	SGD with nesterov momentum ($\mu = 0.99$)
Initial learning rate (lr)	0.01
Training time	15 h/fold
Number of model parameters	210.6 M

We used the dataset and evaluation framework provided by the AortaSeg24 Challenge [5], organized as part of MICCAI 2024. The challenge focuses on multi-class segmentation of the aorta in computed tomography angiography (CTA), including 23 clinically relevant aortic branches and zones. The dataset consists of 100 annotated 3D CTA scans from patients with uncomplicated type B aortic dissection. Each volume was manually annotated by trained researchers and reviewed by an experienced vascular surgeon to ensure clinical accuracy. The annotations include major aortic branches (e.g., renal, iliac, and celiac arteries) and SVS/STS zones, following standard clinical guidelines. All volumes were resampled to an isotropic resolution of $1 \times 1 \times 1$ mm^3 for consistency (Table 1).

Of the 100 scans, 50 were provided for training. The remaining 50 were split between validation and hidden test sets by the organizers. The use of external datasets was not permitted during model development.

3.2 Implementation Details

We implemented our model using the nnU-Net V2 framework [6,7]. Data pre-processing and augmentation followed the default nnU-Net settings. The model was trained and evaluated on an NVIDIA RTX 3090 24GB GPU, using Python 3.10.9, PyTorch 2.2.2, and CUDA 12.1.

To evaluate segmentation performance, we used two standard metrics:

1. **Dice Similarity Coefficient (DSC)** – quantifies volumetric overlap between predicted and reference segmentations.
2. **Normalized Surface Distance (NSD)** – measures the boundary accuracy within a 2 mm tolerance.

3.3 Results on Validation Set

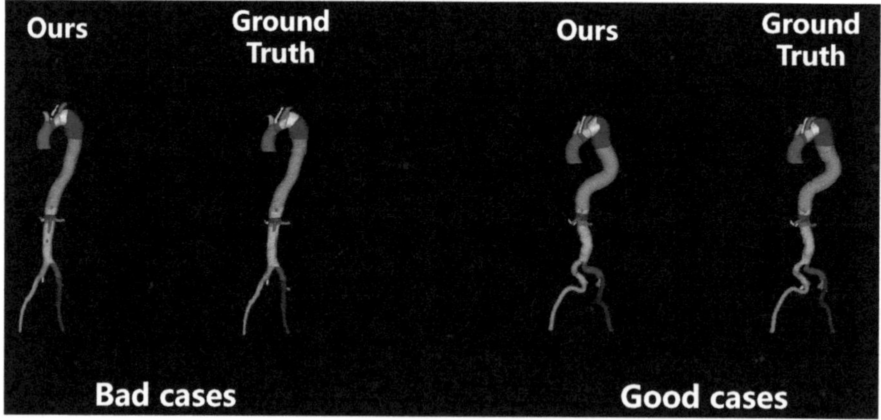

Fig. 3. Qualitative comparison of segmentation results. Left: Bad case showing discontinuities in small vessel categories (red arrows), likely due to limited training data for smaller structures. Right: Good case demonstrating accurate segmentation. (Color figure online)

The hierarchical approach demonstrated faster training convergence and improved segmentation accuracy. As shown in Table 2, our model achieved a

DSC of 70.15 and NSD of 65.87 on the validation set, outperforming the baseline nnU-Net ResEnc M model by 11.65 and 13.56 points, respectively. The clDice metric showed a slight decrease, indicating that while multi-class segmentation improved overall accuracy, it may have introduced some minor inconsistencies in small vessel segmentation.

Table 2. Segmentation Performance on AortaSeg24 Dataset (Epoch 50)

Model	Dice	NSD	clDice
nnU-Net ResEnc M [7]	58.50	52.31	94.29
nnU-Net ResEnc M (w/ HC)	70.15	65.87	93.26
Diff (w/ HC vs. no HC)	+11.65	+13.56	−1.03

Table 3. Inference time comparison between one-stage and two-stage strategies.

Inference Strategy	One Stage (default)	Two Stage ($m = 1, 2, 3, 4$)
Time (s)	115	[22, 61, 98, 127]

As shown in Table 3, the two-stage inference strategy improves speed by up to five times compared to using only Model 2, depending on the expansion factor m.

The qualitative results are shown in Fig. 3. The bad case (left) exhibits fractures in some small vessel categories, which may be attributed to insufficient training data volume and suboptimal generalization capability for smaller anatomical structures. In contrast, the good case (right) demonstrates satisfactory segmentation performance.

3.4   Results on Final Test Set

In this section, discuss the performance of our model on the final test set, as compared to the baseline model, CIS-UNet [4]. Table 4 summarizes the average Dice Similarity Coefficient (DSC) and Normalized Surface Distance (NSD) scores across 40 test images for each anatomical region.

4   Limitations and Future Work

While our hierarchical semantic learning framework significantly improves segmentation accuracy and efficiency, several limitations remain. The model demonstrates suboptimal performance on small vessel categories, primarily due to the

Table 4. Quantitative evaluation on the AortaSeg24 testing dataset. The table reports average Dice and NSD scores across all 40 test cases for each anatomical region. Authors may expand this table to include ablation studies or additional baselines.

Anatomical Region	Our Method		Baseline Method [4]	
	Avg. DSC	Avg. NSD	Avg. DSC	Avg. NSD
Zone 0	0.898	0.81	0.880	0.773
Innominate	0.78	0.832	0.691	0.739
Zone 1	0.644	0.591	0.604	0.560
Left Common Carotid	0.81	0.922	0.743	0.837
Zone 2	0.696	0.582	0.659	0.543
Left Subclavian Artery	0.828	0.906	0.789	0.859
Zone 3	0.691	0.562	0.660	0.517
Zone 4	0.79	0.677	0.746	0.620
Zone 5	0.911	0.88	0.879	0.826
Zone 6	0.715	0.652	0.731	0.678
Celiac Artery	0.675	0.844	0.568	0.728
Zone 7	0.703	0.672	0.699	0.660
SMA	0.748	0.864	0.678	0.782
Zone 8	0.701	0.691	0.664	0.656
Right Renal Artery	0.74	0.897	0.697	0.851
Left Renal Artery	0.69	0.841	0.593	0.742
Zone 9	0.915	0.91	0.879	0.860
Right Common Iliac Artery	0.866	0.921	0.800	0.840
Left Common Iliac Artery	0.863	0.929	0.786	0.842
Right Internal Iliac Artery	0.787	0.919	0.661	0.773
Left Internal Iliac Artery	0.73	0.859	0.640	0.767
Right External Iliac Artery	0.876	0.964	0.789	0.846
Left External Iliac Artery	0.866	0.953	0.783	0.851
Average	**0.779**	**0.812**	**0.723**	**0.746**

limited volume of training data available for these fine structures. Future work will focus on two key directions: (1) enhancing the model's generalization capabilities for smaller anatomical structures, and (2) extending the hierarchical semantic loss framework to a broader range of tasks.

5   Conclusion

We proposed a hierarchical semantic learning framework for multi-class aorta segmentation, which progressively learns anatomical semantics from simpler to more complex structures. The cbDice loss function ensures consistent segmentation across varying vessel diameters. The two-stage inference approach significantly reduces computation time, making the model suitable for real-time clinical applications.

Acknowledgments. We thank all data contributors for making the medical images publicly available, and GrandChallenge for providing the challenge platform. This study was conducted as part of the MICCAI 2024 AortaSeg24 Challenge.

Disclosure of Interests. The authors have no competing interests to declare that are relevant to the content of this article.

Ethical Compliance Statement. All data used was publicly available and anonymized.

References

1. Bengio, Y., Louradour, J., Collobert, R., Weston, J.: Curriculum learning. In: Proceedings of the 26th Annual International Conference on Machine Learning, pp. 41–48 (2009)
2. Bi, W., Kwok, J.T.: Multi-label classification on tree-and DAG-structured hierarchies. In: Proceedings of the 28th International Conference on Machine Learning (ICML 2011), pp. 17–24 (2011)
3. Giunchiglia, E., Lukasiewicz, T.: Coherent hierarchical multi-label classification networks. Adv. Neural. Inf. Process. Syst. **33**, 9662–9673 (2020)
4. Imran, M., et al.: CIS-UNet: multi-class segmentation of the aorta in computed tomography angiography via context-aware shifted window self-attention. Comput. Med. Imaging Graph **118**, 102470 (2024)
5. Imran, M., et al.: Multi-class segmentation of aortic branches and zones in computed tomography angiography: the aortaseg24 challenge. arXiv preprint arXiv:2502.05330 (2025)
6. Isensee, F., Jaeger, P.F., Kohl, S.A., Petersen, J., Maier-Hein, K.H.: nnu-net: a self-configuring method for deep learning-based biomedical image segmentation. Nat. Methods **18**(2), 203–211 (2021)
7. Isensee, F., et al.: nnu-net revisited: a call for rigorous validation in 3d medical image segmentation. arXiv preprint arXiv:2404.09556 (2024)
8. Li, L., Wang, W., Zhou, T., Quan, R., Yang, Y.: Semantic hierarchy-aware segmentation. IEEE Trans. Pattern Anal. Mach. Intell. (2023)
9. Li, T., Sun, Q., Fan, L., He, K.: Fractal generative models. arXiv preprint arXiv:2502.17437 (2025)
10. Lin, T.Y., Goyal, P., Girshick, R., He, K., Dollár, P.: Focal loss for dense object detection. In: Proceedings of the IEEE International Conference on Computer Vision, pp. 2980–2988 (2017)
11. Shi, P., Hu, J., Yang, Y., Gao, Z., Liu, W., Ma, T.: Centerline boundary dice loss for vascular segmentation. In: International Conference on Medical Image Computing and Computer-Assisted Intervention, pp. 46–56. Springer (2024)

12. Wang, X., Chen, Y., Zhu, W.: A survey on curriculum learning. IEEE Trans. Pattern Anal. Mach. Intell. **44**(9), 4555–4576 (2021)
13. Wasserthal, J., et al.: Totalsegmentator: robust segmentation of 104 anatomic structures in CT images. Radiol. Artif. Intell. **5**(5) (2023)
14. Wehrmann, J., Cerri, R., Barros, R.: Hierarchical multi-label classification networks. In: International Conference on Machine Learning, pp. 5075–5084. PMLR (2018)

U-Net-Based Segmentation of Aortic Branches and Zones in CTA Scans

Thanh Bong Nguyen[1(✉)] , DongJin Shin[1,2], JiWoo Park[1,2] ,
Matthew Choi[1,2] , KwangHyun Uhm[1,3] , and Sung-Jea Ko[1,2]

[1] MedAI, Seoul, Korea
contact@medai.im
[2] Korea University, Seoul, Korea
[3] Gachon University, Seongnam, Korea
https://medai.im/en

Abstract. Accurate segmentation of aortic zones and branches in computed tomography angiography (CTA) is essential for diagnosis and treatment planning of aortic diseases. In this paper, we present a 3D multi-class segmentation approach based on a U-Net architecture enhanced with ResNet blocks in both the encoder and decoder. The model was implemented using the nnU-Net framework with standardized preprocessing, including Z-score normalization, isotropic resampling, and patch-based sampling, alongside data augmentation techniques to improve generalization. We evaluated our method on the AortaSeg24 challenge dataset, which consists of 50 annotated CTA scans. On the final testing set of 40 images, our model achieved an average Dice Similarity Coefficient (DSC) of **0.773 ± 0.028** and an average Normalized Surface Distance (NSD) of **0.805 ± 0.038**, outperforming the baseline CIS-UNet model (DSC: 0.723 ± 0.058, NSD: 0.746 ± 0.067). Our method performed especially well in segmenting major aortic zones and iliac arteries, while minor label confusion was observed in smaller distal branches. These results demonstrate the effectiveness of using residual connections within the U-Net framework for detailed and anatomically consistent aortic segmentation.

Keywords: Aorta segmentation · 3D segmentation · Residual UNet

1 Introduction

The aorta is the largest artery in the human body, responsible for transporting oxygenated blood from the heart to the brain, limbs, and vital organs. Aortic diseases such as aneurysms, dissections, and atherosclerosis can have life-threatening consequences, requiring rapid diagnosis and precise treatment planning. Computed tomography angiography (CTA) is widely used in clinical practice for evaluating the aortic anatomy due to its high-resolution imaging and strong vascular contrast [1]. Accurate segmentation of the aorta and its branches

M. Imran et al. (Eds.): AortaSeg 2024, LNCS 16399, pp. 23–34, 2026.
https://doi.org/10.1007/978-3-032-14246-7_3

from CTA is essential for quantitative analysis, treatment planning, and post-operative assessment. However, manual segmentation is labor-intensive, time-consuming, and prone to observer variability, especially in complex anatomical regions or diseased vessels.

In recent years, deep learning has shown promise in automating medical image segmentation tasks, including aortic segmentation in CTA. Convolutional neural networks (CNNs) have been widely adopted to segment the aorta and other cardiovascular structures with high accuracy [9–14]. Despite these advances, most existing models perform binary segmentation of the main aortic lumen, offering limited support for anatomical detail such as specific aortic branches or zones. To address this, transformer-based models like CIS-UNet have been proposed to capture broader contextual information via shifted window self-attention and have demonstrated improved performance in multi-class segmentation tasks [3]. However, challenges remain in handling anatomical variability, vessel tortuosity, and class imbalance across different zones and branches. In response to the need for a standardized benchmark, the AortaSeg24 Challenge was introduced at MICCAI 2024, offering a multi-institutional dataset and evaluation framework to support fine-grained segmentation of aortic branches and zones in CTA [4]. This initiative builds upon earlier work emphasizing the clinical value of regional aortic segmentation, such as that by Krebs et al., who used zone-wise segmentation for volumetric assessment in acute type B dissection [7].

In this study, we propose a fully automated method for multi-class segmentation of the aorta and its branches using the Unet architecture with residual blocks. Our approach leverages the hierarchical feature extraction and residual connections of model to effectively capture complex vascular structures. To further improve anatomical consistency, we integrate the Skeleton Recall Loss function [6], which encourages preservation of the aortic centerline and penalizes topological errors. This combination enables our model to segment both major and peripheral vascular regions with high accuracy, even in the presence of disease or anatomical variation. We evaluate our method on the AortaSeg24 dataset and demonstrate its effectiveness in producing reliable, fine-grained multi-class segmentations suitable for clinical and research applications.

2   Method

2.1   Network Architecture

We employ a 3D U-Net-style architecture [8] augmented with residual connections, following the design principles of ResNet [2], for multi-class segmentation of aortic zones and branches in CTA volumes. The model which is shown in Fig. 1 is structured as an encoder-decoder network, where both the encoder and decoder utilize residual blocks to facilitate deep feature learning. This design enables effective hierarchical representation of anatomical structures while preserving spatial detail critical for vascular segmentation.

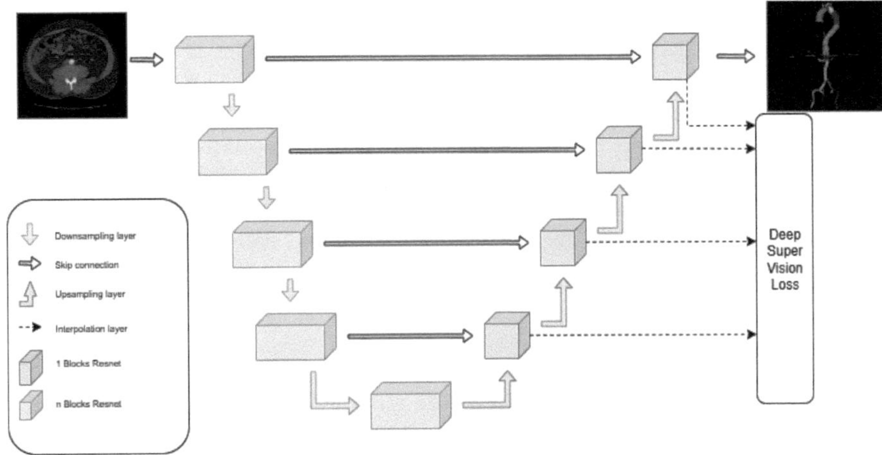

Fig. 1. Network architecture designed as a U-Net-style encoder-decoder structure enhanced with ResNet blocks in both the encoder and decoder. Downsampling is performed via strided convolutions, while upsampling is handled through interpolation and convolution layers. Skip connections fuse encoder and decoder features at each resolution level. Deep supervision is applied at multiple decoder stages to improve gradient flow and facilitate convergence.

2.2   Pre-processing

Data preprocessing includes intensity normalization, spatial resampling, and patch-based sampling to reduce memory consumption. All images are resampled to a uniform voxel spacing derived from the training data, and non-zero regions are cropped to restrict computation to anatomically relevant areas. Intensity normalization is applied on a per-image basis to standardize voxel intensities across scans.

In addition, we systematically explored several preprocessing strategies to further enhance model performance. For intensity normalization, we compared *range normalization* (min-max scaling) and *Z-score normalization*, with the latter showing consistently superior results.

To improve sampling efficiency and class balance during training, we implemented a *random sub-sampling* strategy. In each epoch, non-background voxels were randomly selected for each label class, and 3D sub-volumes of size $w \times h \times d$ were extracted around these points. This approach ensures that training patches are centered on anatomically meaningful structures, allowing the network to focus on underrepresented classes while minimizing the influence of irrelevant background.

2.3   Encoder

The encoder consists of multiple hierarchical stages, where each stage contains a sequence of ResNet blocks. Each block is composed of two 3D convolutional layers, followed by batch normalization and non-linear activation functions. By stacking multiple ResNet blocks at each level, the encoder is able to progressively capture complex spatial features while deepening the receptive field. The use of ResNet-style skip connections within these blocks facilitates stable gradient flow and mitigates vanishing gradient issues, especially in deeper layers. Downsampling is performed via strided convolutions (stride = 2), reducing spatial resolution while increasing feature dimensionality. This hierarchical structure allows the network to learn increasingly abstract and robust representations of the aortic anatomy as depth increases.

2.4   Decoder

The decoder mirrors the encoder structure and also employs a residual block at each resolution level to refine feature representations after upsampling. Feature maps are progressively upsampled using transposed convolutions or interpolation followed by convolution, restoring the spatial dimensions to match the original input. Skip connections between encoder and decoder levels help recover fine-grained spatial details lost during downsampling. The use of residual blocks in the decoder ensures consistent feature refinement and facilitates better reconstruction of intricate structures such as narrow and tortuous vessels.

To generate the final segmentation output, a $1 \times 1 \times 1$ convolutional layer is applied at the end of each decoder level. These layers reduce the number of feature channels to match the number of anatomical classes, enabling voxel-wise classification without altering the spatial resolution. By aggregating local features at each voxel, this design maintains anatomical precision while enabling efficient mapping from deep features to class labels. It also supports deep supervision by allowing the segmentation loss to be computed directly from the decoder output, improving convergence and segmentation accuracy.

3   Experiments

3.1   Dataset and Evaluation Metrics

We utilized the dataset and evaluation framework provided by the AortaSeg24 Challenge [4], organized in conjunction with MICCAI 2024. The challenge targets the task of multi-class segmentation of the aorta and its branches in computed tomography angiography (CTA), encompassing 23 clinically relevant anatomical labels. The dataset comprises 100 annotated 3D CTA scans from patients with uncomplicated type B aortic dissection. Each scan was manually segmented by trained annotators and reviewed by a board-certified vascular surgeon to ensure clinical accuracy. The annotation protocol includes key aortic branches (e.g., renal, iliac, and celiac arteries) as well as SVS/STS-defined zones, in accordance with established clinical guidelines. All volumes were resampled to an isotropic resolution of $1 \times 1 \times 1$ mm^3 for consistency across the dataset.

Out of the 100 scans, 50 were released for training. The remaining 50 were retained by the organizers and split between a validation set and a hidden test set. The use of external data was not permitted during model development to ensure fair benchmarking.

Segmentation performance was assessed using two standard evaluation metrics:

1. **Dice Similarity Coefficient (DSC)** – measures volumetric overlap between the predicted segmentation and the ground truth.
2. **Normalized Surface Distance (NSD)** – quantifies boundary alignment by computing the proportion of surface points within a $2\,\mathrm{mm}$ tolerance.

3.2   Implementation Details

Data Preprocessing. We conducted a series of preprocessing steps to prepare the CTA volumes for model training. First, we clipped the intensity values of each image to a fixed range of $[-175, 450]$ Hounsfield units to suppress irrelevant background and enhance vessel contrast. We then evaluated two normalization methods—range normalization (min-max scaling after clipping) and Z-score normalization—and quantitatively compared their effects on segmentation performance. As shown in Table 1, Z-score normalization yielded higher Dice scores in 16 out of 23 anatomical labels and improved the average Dice score from 0.7562 (CTnorm) to 0.7619. This supports our choice of Z-score normalization as the final preprocessing method, as it led to more stable training and consistently better segmentation results, particularly in smaller or more variable structures.

Following normalization, all volumes were resampled to a uniform voxel spacing of $1 \times 1 \times 1$ mm to ensure consistency in spatial resolution across the dataset. The resampled images were then cropped to extract patches centered around the non-zero foreground, reducing memory usage and focusing the network on regions of anatomical interest.

To increase the diversity and robustness of the training data, we applied several data augmentation techniques. These included random flipping and random rotation along all three axes, each applied with a probability of 0.2. Additionally, we used random intensity scaling and shifting, each with a probability of 0.1, to simulate brightness and contrast variability. These augmentations help prevent overfitting and improve the generalizability of the model to unseen data.

Environment Settings. The development environment and software requirements are summarized in Table 2.

Training Protocols. The dataset consisted of 50 contrast-enhanced CTA volumes, which were divided into 40 for training and 10 for testing. This split provided a balanced framework for evaluating the model's ability to generalize to unseen data. Model training was conducted using the `nnU-Net` framework [5], which offers a robust and adaptive pipeline for medical image segmentation. Details of the training configuration and results are summarized in Table 3.

Table 1. Dice coefficient comparison between CTnorm and Z-score normalization across 23 anatomical regions. Higher scores per region are highlighted in bold.

Anatomical Region	CT norm	Z-score
Zone 0	0.9204	**0.9154**
Innominate	**0.7113**	0.6924
Zone 1	0.6169	**0.6305**
Left Common Carotid	0.8053	**0.8264**
Zone 2	**0.7407**	0.7290
Left Subclavian Artery	0.8150	**0.8301**
Zone 3	**0.7439**	0.7216
Zone 4	0.8321	**0.8509**
Zone 5	0.9077	**0.9165**
Zone 6	**0.6797**	0.6464
Celiac Artery	0.6844	**0.7227**
Zone 7	**0.6857**	0.6544
SMA	0.7838	**0.7935**
Zone 8	0.7509	**0.7593**
Right Renal Artery	**0.7238**	0.7167
Left Renal Artery	**0.7177**	0.7014
Zone 9	0.8897	**0.9045**
Right Common Iliac Artery	0.7962	**0.8127**
Left Common Iliac Artery	0.7603	**0.7921**
Right Internal Iliac Artery	0.6013	**0.6196**
Left Internal Iliac Artery	0.5937	**0.6297**
Right External Iliac Artery	**0.8296**	0.8273
Left External Iliac Artery	0.8020	**0.8300**
Average	0.7562	**0.7619**

Table 2. Development environments and requirements.

System	Ubuntu 18.04.5 LTS or Windows 10
CPU	Intel(R) Core(TM) i9-7900X CPU@3.30GHz
RAM	16×4 GB; 2.67MT/s
GPU (number and type)	NVIDIA GeForce RTX 3090
CUDA version	11.0
Programming language	Python 3.10
Deep learning framework	torch 2.0, torchvision 0.2.2

Table 3. Training protocols.

Batch size	2
Patch size	$256 \times 160 \times 160$
Total epochs	1000
Optimizer	AdamW with a weight decay of 1.0×10^{-5}
Loss function	DiceCE
Initial learning rate (lr)	0.01
Lr decay schedule	PolynomialLR
Training time	40 h
Number of model parameters	102 M[a]
Number of flops	19.5 G[b]

[a] https://github.com/sksq96/pytorch-summary.
[b] https://github.com/facebookresearch/fvcore.

4   Results and Discussion

4.1   Qualitative Results on Validation Set

From the initial dataset of 50 CTA volumes, 40 were used for training and 10 for validation. We selected representative cases from the validation set to illustrate both successful and challenging segmentation outcomes, as shown in Fig. 2. Our model performs well in segmenting the major aortic zones, particularly Zones 0, 5, and 9, which are large and anatomically consistent across subjects. In these regions, the predicted segmentations closely align with the ground truth boundaries, capturing both shape and class label accurately.

However, failure cases typically occur in smaller and more variable vascular branches. The most frequent mis-segmentation is observed in Zones 6, 7, and 8 (labels 20–23), where the model often confuses adjacent anatomical structures. This is likely due to the limited spatial resolution, high anatomical variability, and severe class imbalance across labels. In these cases, although the overall aortic shape is preserved, the classification of finer branches is often incorrect. For example, left and right internal iliac arteries are sometimes mislabeled or partially missed, likely due to their small size and close proximity to each other and to the external iliac arteries.

4.2   Qualitative Results on Validation Set

Figure 2 illustrates two representative examples from the validation set. The left side of each pair shows the ground truth segmentation, while the right side shows the corresponding model prediction. The top row represents a good case, where the model successfully segmented all major aortic regions and branches. This sample achieved a high Dice score of 0.8396, with nearly perfect alignment across zones and arteries. The boundaries and class assignments in this example show strong agreement with the ground truth, indicating the model's ability to preserve aortic topology and anatomical consistency in well-represented cases.

The bottom row depicts a challenging case with a dice score of 0.6074, particularly in the segmentation of smaller distal branches. While the overall aortic shape was well preserved, the model frequently confused closely located or low-contrast regions, resulting in incorrect class assignments. This is especially visible in the last four anatomical labels, such as Zones 6, 7, and 8, and the internal iliac arteries. Such failures are likely due to class imbalance and anatomical variation across patients. These structures are often small, thin, and difficult to differentiate from adjacent vessels, contributing to reduced Dice and NSD scores in these categories.

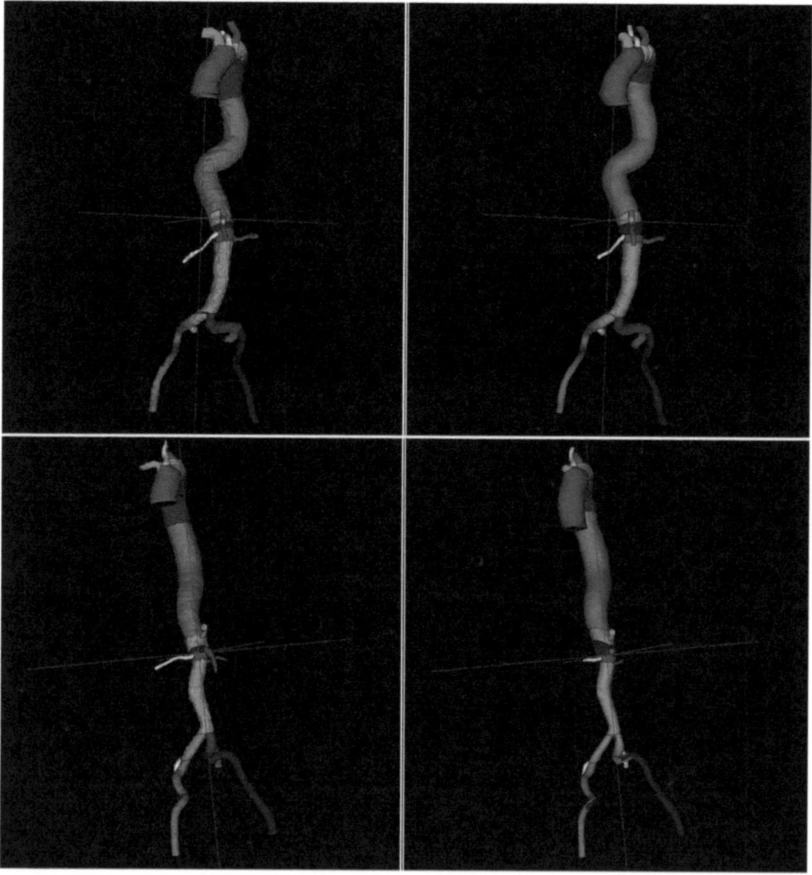

Fig. 2. Qualitative segmentation results. **Top:** successful case with accurate segmentation (Dice = 0.8396). **Bottom:** failure case, showing label confusion and misclassification (Dice = 0.6074). In both rows, **left** is ground truth, and **right** is model prediction.

4.3   Results on Final Testing Set

The performance of our method on the AortaSeg24 final testing set is summarized in Table 4, which compares the average Dice Similarity Coefficient (DSC) and Normalized Surface Distance (NSD) scores across 40 test subjects against the baseline model, CIS-UNet [3]. Our method achieved an overall average Dice score of **0.773 ± 0.028** and an NSD of **0.805 ± 0.038**, outperforming the baseline model, which scored **0.723 ± 0.058** and **0.746 ± 0.067**, respectively. The improvements are consistent across nearly all anatomical regions, including both major zones (e.g., Zone 0, Zone 5, Zone 9) and smaller branches such as the renal and iliac arteries. Notably, significant performance gains were observed in zones and vessels where anatomical consistency and shape continuity

Table 4. Quantitative evaluation on the AortaSeg24 testing dataset. The table reports average Dice and NSD scores (mean ± standard deviation) across all 40 test cases for each anatomical region. Authors may expand this table to include ablation studies or additional baselines.

Anatomical Region	Our Method		Baseline Method [3]	
	Avg. DSC	Avg. NSD	Avg. DSC	Avg. NSD
Zone 0	0.894 ± 0.053	0.798 ± 0.122	0.880 ± 0.064	0.773 ± 0.119
Innominate	0.784 ± 0.150	0.842 ± 0.171	0.691 ± 0.164	0.739 ± 0.175
Zone 1	0.620 ± 0.193	0.574 ± 0.174	0.604 ± 0.164	0.560 ± 0.150
Left Common Carotid	0.816 ± 0.055	0.924 ± 0.056	0.743 ± 0.108	0.837 ± 0.117
Zone 2	0.690 ± 0.129	0.578 ± 0.150	0.659 ± 0.143	0.543 ± 0.153
Left Subclavian Artery	0.827 ± 0.070	0.906 ± 0.085	0.789 ± 0.115	0.859 ± 0.115
Zone 3	0.697 ± 0.153	0.569 ± 0.156	0.660 ± 0.171	0.517 ± 0.181
Zone 4	0.786 ± 0.108	0.663 ± 0.124	0.746 ± 0.122	0.620 ± 0.139
Zone 5	0.906 ± 0.032	0.865 ± 0.077	0.879 ± 0.054	0.826 ± 0.096
Zone 6	0.706 ± 0.130	0.643 ± 0.166	0.731 ± 0.123	0.678 ± 0.164
Celiac Artery	0.660 ± 0.163	0.837 ± 0.154	0.568 ± 0.178	0.728 ± 0.168
Zone 7	0.699 ± 0.133	0.663 ± 0.153	0.699 ± 0.116	0.660 ± 0.146
SMA	0.743 ± 0.102	0.861 ± 0.109	0.678 ± 0.131	0.782 ± 0.135
Zone 8	0.703 ± 0.125	0.691 ± 0.144	0.664 ± 0.160	0.656 ± 0.160
Right Renal Artery	0.743 ± 0.118	0.896 ± 0.124	0.697 ± 0.142	0.851 ± 0.140
Left Renal Artery	0.690 ± 0.165	0.841 ± 0.164	0.593 ± 0.199	0.742 ± 0.216
Zone 9	0.914 ± 0.042	0.911 0.100	0.879 ± 0.081	0.860 ± 0.130
Right Common Iliac Artery	0.849 ± 0.104	0.902 ± 0.112	0.800 ± 0.132	0.840 ± 0.148
Left Common Iliac Artery	0.860 ± 0.048	0.923 ± 0.077	0.786 ± 0.135	0.842 ± 0.164
Right Internal Iliac Artery	0.787 ± 0.091	0.920 ± 0.094	0.661 ± 0.167	0.773 ± 0.179
Left Internal Iliac Artery	0.742 ± 0.130	0.875 ± 0.130	0.640 ± 0.197	0.767 ± 0.205
Right External Iliac Artery	0.827 ± 0.134	0.916 ± 0.137	0.789 ± 0.134	0.846 ± 0.143
Left External Iliac Artery	0.836 ± 0.122	0.919 ± 0.132	0.783 ± 0.151	0.851 ± 0.160
Overall	**0.773 ± 0.028**	**0.805 ± 0.038**	**0.723 ± 0.058**	**0.746 ± 0.067**

are critical—demonstrating the advantage of integrating our architectural modifications. The only exception is **Zone 6**, where CIS-UNet slightly outperformed our model. This discrepancy may be attributed to the anatomical complexity and variability of this zone, as well as potential class imbalance during training. Despite this, our method still achieved competitive performance in Zone 6, and surpassed the baseline in all remaining 22 anatomical labels. These results validate the effectiveness of our design in improving segmentation accuracy and surface alignment, especially for structurally complex vascular regions.

4.4 Limitation and Future Work

While our model achieved strong overall performance on the AortaSeg24 dataset, a detailed analysis reveals both strengths and limitations. The proposed U-Net with ResNet blocks performed consistently well on large and clearly defined anatomical zones, particularly Zone 0, Zone 5, and Zone 9, as well as in the common iliac arteries. These regions typically exhibit less anatomical variation and are well represented in the training data, making them easier for the model to learn.

In contrast, segmentation accuracy was lower for smaller, more variable, or anatomically ambiguous regions—such as Zone 6, internal iliac arteries, and distal branches—where misclassification and label confusion were more frequent. These errors can be attributed to class imbalance, close spatial proximity between adjacent vessels, and limited contextual information within cropped patches. Additionally, although Z-score normalization improved performance slightly compared to range-based normalization, its effect was modest in challenging regions.

To address these limitations, future work could focus on several directions:

- **Class imbalance handling:** Incorporating class-aware sampling or loss re-weighting strategies may improve segmentation of underrepresented structures.
- **Improved contextual modeling:** Adding attention mechanisms or hybrid transformer-CNN modules could enhance global feature representation and reduce confusion in overlapping or adjacent vessels.
- **Geometric priors:** Integrating anatomical priors, such as centerline constraints or topological regularization, may improve structural consistency in complex vascular regions.
- **Clinical downstream tasks:** Extending this work to include automatic measurements, centerline extraction, and risk scoring could facilitate end-to-end clinical workflows.
- **Generalizability:** Future experiments on external, multi-institutional datasets are needed to evaluate the model's robustness and clinical readiness.

Overall, our findings suggest that residual U-Net architectures can serve as a strong foundation for high-resolution vascular segmentation, while leaving room for targeted improvements in anatomically difficult regions.

5   Conclusion

In this study, we presented an automated 3D multi-class segmentation method for aortic zones and branches in CTA scans. Our model is based on a U-Net architecture enhanced with ResNet blocks in both the encoder and decoder, enabling effective feature extraction and improved gradient flow. The network was trained using the nnU-Net framework with optimized preprocessing, including Z-score normalization and patch-based sampling. Evaluated on the AortaSeg24 challenge dataset, our method achieved an average Dice score of **0.773 ± 0.028** and NSD of **0.805 ± 0.038** on the final testing set, outperforming the CIS-UNet baseline. The model demonstrated strong performance in major aortic regions and robust generalization across a wide range of anatomical structures. These results highlight the potential of residual U-Net architectures for clinically useful, fine-grained aortic segmentation, reducing the need for manual annotation in vascular analysis workflows.

Acknowledgements. We thank all data contributors for making the medical images publicly available, and GrandChallenge for providing the challenge platform. This work was supported by Artificial intelligence industrial convergence cluster development project funded by the Ministry of Science and ICT (MSIT, Korea) & Gwangju Metropolitan City and was supported by the Technology development Program (RS-2024-00460263) funded by the Ministry of SMEs and Startups (MSS, Korea).

Disclosure of Interests. The authors have no competing interests to declare that are relevant to the content of this article.

Ethical Compliance Statement. All data used was publicly available and anonymized.

References

1. Cademartiri, F., van der Lugt, A., Luccichenti, G., Pavone, P., Krestin, G.P.: Parameters affecting bolus geometry in CTA: a review. J. Comput. Assist. Tomogr. **26**(4), 598–607 (2002)
2. He, K., Zhang, X., Ren, S., Sun, J.: Identity mappings in deep residual networks. In: Leibe, B., Matas, J., Sebe, N., Welling, M. (eds.) ECCV 2016. LNCS, vol. 9908, pp. 630–645. Springer, Cham (2016). https://doi.org/10.1007/978-3-319-46493-0_38
3. Imran, M., et al.: CIS-UNet: multi-class segmentation of the aorta in computed tomography angiography via context-aware shifted window self-attention. Comput. Med. Imaging Graph. **118**, 102470 (2024)
4. Imran, M., et al.: Multi-class segmentation of aortic branches and zones in computed tomography angiography: the aortaseg24 challenge. arXiv preprint arXiv:2502.05330 (2025)
5. Isensee, F., Jaeger, P.F., Kohl, S.A., Petersen, J., Maier-Hein, K.H.: nnu-net: a self-configuring method for deep learning-based biomedical image segmentation. Nat. Methods **18**(2), 203–211 (2021)

6. Kirchhoff, Y., Rokuss, M., Roy, S., et al.: Skeleton recall loss for connectivity conserving and resource efficient segmentation of thin tubular structures. In: European Conference on Computer Vision (2024)
7. Krebs, J.R., et al.: Volumetric analysis of acute uncomplicated type b aortic dissection using an automated deep learning aortic zone segmentation model. J. Vasc. Surg. **80**(4), 1025–1034 (2024)
8. Ronneberger, O., Fischer, P., Brox, T.: U-Net: convolutional networks for biomedical image segmentation. In: Navab, N., Hornegger, J., Wells, W.M., Frangi, A.F. (eds.) MICCAI 2015. LNCS, vol. 9351, pp. 234–241. Springer, Cham (2015). https://doi.org/10.1007/978-3-319-24574-4_28
9. Sieren, M.M., et al.: Automated segmentation and quantification of the healthy and diseased aorta in CT angiographies using a dedicated deep learning approach. Eur. Radiol. **32**(1), 690–701 (2022)
10. Uhm, K.H., et al.: Exploring 3D U-Net training configurations and post-processing strategies for the MICCAI 2023 kidney and tumor segmentation challenge. In: Kidney and Kidney Tumor Segmentation, pp. 8–13. Springer, Cham (2024)
11. Uhm, K.H., Jung, S.W., Choi, M.H., Hong, S.H., Ko, S.J.: A unified multi-phase CT synthesis and classification framework for kidney cancer diagnosis with incomplete data. IEEE J. Biomed. Health Inform. **26**(12), 6093–6104 (2022)
12. Uhm, K.H., Jung, S.W., Hong, S.H., Ko, S.J.: Lesion-aware cross-phase attention network for renal tumor subtype classification on multi-phase CT scans. Comput. Biol. Med. **178**, 108746 (2024)
13. Uhm, K.H., Shin, H.K., Cho, H.J., Jung, S.W., Ko, S.J.: 3D reconstruction based on multi-phase CT for kidney cancer surgery. In: 2023 International Technical Conference on Circuits/Systems, Computers, and Communications (ITC-CSCC), pp. 1–2 (2023)
14. Uhm, K.H., et al.: Deep learning for end-to-end kidney cancer diagnosis on multiphase abdominal computed tomography. NPJ Precis. Onc. **5**(54) (2021)

Anatomically Guided Two-Stage 3D Aorta Segmentation in CT Angiography

Chanwoong Lee[1,2], Jaehee Chun[3], and Jin Sung Kim[1,2,3]($\boxtimes$)

[1] Department of Radiation Oncology, Yonsei Cancer Center, Heavy Ion Therapy Research Institute, Yonsei University College of Medicine, Seoul, South Korea
`Jinsung@yuhs.ac`
[2] Medical Physics and Biomedical Engineering Lab (MPBEL), Yonsei University College of Medicine, Seoul, South Korea
[3] Oncosoft Inc., Seoul, South Korea
`http://mpbel.yonsei.ac.kr`

Abstract. Accurate segmentation of the aorta and its 23 substructures is crucial for planning endovascular interventions and treating aortic pathologies. However, deep learning approaches often face practical limits when handling high-resolution 3D computed tomography angiography (CTA). We propose a two-stage framework, *AortaSeg*, which integrates a 2D object detector with a 3D patch-based segmentation network to reduce memory usage without sacrificing accuracy. Stage 1 localizes anatomical regions using a YOLOv7-based detector guided by reference organs from TotalSegmentator, and Stage 2 applies section-specific 3D DynUNets to cropped sub-volumes. This modular design enables efficient processing of large CTA volumes and improves focus on challenging substructures. On the hidden test set of the MICCAI 2024 AortaSeg Challenge, AortaSeg achieved a Dice Similarity Coefficient (DSC) of 0.767 $\pm$ 0.032 and a Normalized Surface Distance (NSD) of 0.797 $\pm$ 0.037, ranking 5th among 32 teams, demonstrating a favorable balance between performance and efficiency.

Keywords: Aorta segmentation · Deep learning · Object detection · DynUNet · Two-stage learning

1 Introduction

The aorta is the largest artery in the body and supplies oxygenated blood to the upper extremities, abdomen, pelvis, and lower extremities. Pathologies of the aorta and its main branches—including dissection, aneurysm, and atherosclerotic disease—can be limb- or life-threatening and often require prompt surgical evaluation and treatment [4]. Advances in computed tomography angiography (CTA) and endovascular therapies have reshaped clinical management.

Accurate segmentation of the aorta and its branches is essential for endovascular planning. Recent progress in automated segmentation has been driven by deep learning, which helps reduce inter- and intra-observer variability and improves reproducibility [2,3,7,9]. Nevertheless, deploying state-of-the-art 3D

M. Imran et al. (Eds.): AortaSeg 2024, LNCS 16399, pp. 35–46, 2026.
https://doi.org/10.1007/978-3-032-14246-7_4

models in practice can be difficult due to the substantial memory required by high-resolution volumes on a single graphics processing unit (GPU).

We address this constraint with a simple principle: *localize first, then segment*. Our framework uses (1) a 2D detector to localize anatomically meaningful regions and (2) region-wise 3D networks for fine segmentation within cropped sub-volumes. This two-stage pipeline concentrates computation where it matters, enabling high-resolution processing while keeping memory demands manageable. In what follows, we describe the anatomical zoning and model design, and show that the approach yields competitive accuracy on the AortaSeg24 Challenge.

2   Method

2.1   Pre-processing and Anatomical Zoning

To ensure consistency with the detection model, all CT images were resampled to a 512×512 axial resolution. Larger images were center-cropped and smaller ones zero-padded. Intensities were clipped to the Hounsfield Unit (HU) range of $[-500, 1000]$ and normalized to $[0, 255]$ for 2D detection compatibility.

For spatial decomposition, the aorta and its branches were divided into three anatomical sections using reference organ locations automatically segmented with TotalSegmentator. Each section corresponds to specific labels and boundaries along the Right–Left, Anterior–Posterior, and Inferior–Superior axes. This design enables localized detection and segmentation, improving memory efficiency and mitigating class imbalance. Figure 1 shows the 3D distribution of the 23 targets; Tables 1 and 2 summarize label assignments and boundary definitions.

Table 1. Label grouping by anatomical section. Zones and branches are assigned to one of three sections for region-wise detection and segmentation.

Section	Anatomical Region
1	Zone 0, Innominate, Zone 1, Left Common Carotid
	Zone 2, Left Subclavian Artery, Zone 3, Zone 4
2	Zone 5, Zone 6, Celiac Artery, Zone 7
	SMA, Zone 8, Right Renal Artery, Left Renal Artery
3	Zone 9, Zone 10 R (Right Common Iliac Artery),
	Zone 10 L (Left Common Iliac Artery),
	Right Internal Iliac Artery, Left Internal Iliac Artery,
	Zone 11 R (Right External Iliac Artery),
	Zone 11 L (Left External Iliac Artery)

2.2   Model Component 1: Network Architecture

Our framework comprises a 2D detector and a 3D segmentation module. As illustrated in Fig. 2, Stage 1 identifies regions of interest (ROIs) from anatom-

Table 2. Reference-organ boundaries used to define each section.

Section	Right–Left	Anterior–Posterior	Inferior–Superior
1	Right scapula – Left scapula	Sternum – Scapula	Scapula – Heart
2	Left hip – Right hip	Sternum – Scapula	Hip – Heart
3	Left hip – Right hip	Sternum – Scapula	Hip – Kidney

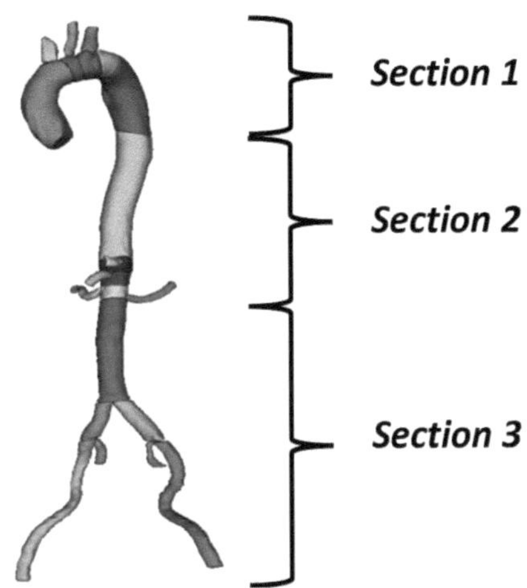

Fig. 1. 3D visualization of the aorta and branches divided into three anatomical sections. Colors denote segmentation labels. The zoning guides both detection and region-wise segmentation (see Tables 1 and 2).

ical context; Stage 2 applies section-specific 3D networks to each cropped subvolume. The design was informed by our prior experience in region-wise training for head-and-neck anatomy [8], which improved accuracy and generalization.

Stage 1: Object Detection (YOLOv7). We employ YOLOv7 [10] on axial slices of resampled CTA. Bounding boxes are derived from normal organs segmented by TotalSegmentator [11] to localize three subregions. The detector uses re-parameterized modules for efficient feature reuse. Training details are in Table 3. Detected boxes guide 3D crops for the next stage.

Stage 2: Segmentation (DynUNet). For fine segmentation we use DynUNet from MONAI [1]. Patch sizes and spacings were tuned per section to balance resolution and memory. Each subregion is processed by a dedicated model; predictions are aggregated into the final multi-class map (Table 4).

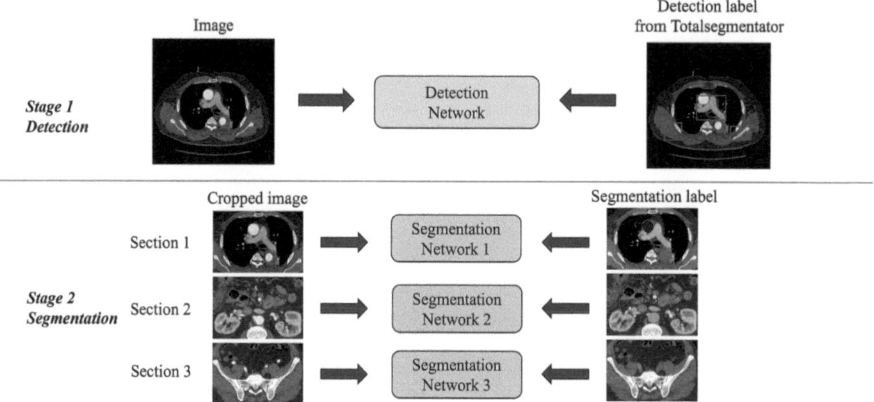

Fig. 2. Overview of the AortaSeg framework. Stage 1 (YOLOv7) identifies ROI bounding boxes using anatomical context. Stage 2 applies three section-specific 3D DynUNets to cropped sub-volumes. Outputs are fused to reconstruct the full aortic segmentation.

2.3   Inference Process

At inference, the detector first produces bounding boxes for the three sections. Sub-volumes are cropped accordingly and sent to their respective 3D networks. The region-wise outputs are then merged to obtain the final segmentation (Fig. 3). This modular pipeline reduces memory burden and focuses each model on anatomically coherent structures.

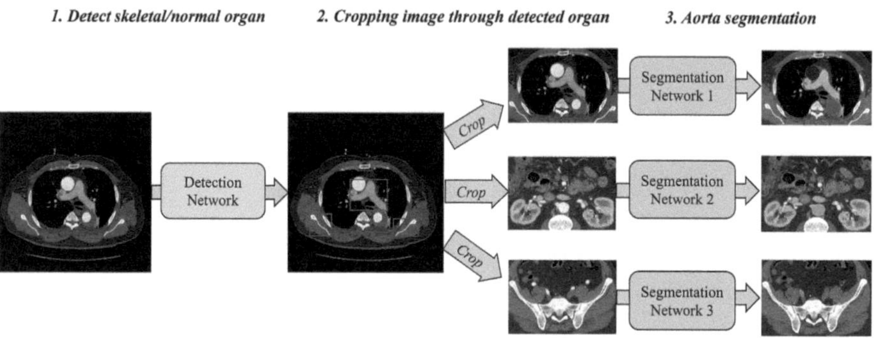

Fig. 3. Inference pipeline. The detector localizes three anatomical sections, enabling cropped sub-volumes for section-wise 3D segmentation. Region predictions are aggregated into a final multi-class map.

3   Experiments

3.1   Dataset and Evaluation Protocol

We used the AortaSeg24 Challenge dataset and evaluation framework [6], focused on multi-class segmentation of 23 aortic branches and zones in CTA. The dataset contains 100 annotated 3D scans from patients with uncomplicated type B aortic dissection. Each volume was manually annotated and reviewed by an experienced vascular surgeon. All scans were resampled to $1 \times 1 \times 1\,\mathrm{mm}^3$. Fifty scans were released for training; the remainder were split by the organizers into validation and hidden test sets. External data were not permitted.

We report Dice Similarity Coefficient (DSC) for volumetric overlap and Normalized Surface Distance (NSD) within a 2 mm tolerance.

3.2   Implementation Details

Data Preprocessing. All CT images were resampled to 512×512 in-plane resolution. Larger images were center-cropped; smaller ones were zero-padded. For detection, intensities were clipped to $[-500, 1000]$ HU and normalized to $[0, 255]$. For segmentation, we used a two-channel input: Channel 0 used $[-1024, 3071]$ HU; Channel 1 emphasized soft tissue in $[-200, 300]$ HU (Fig. 4).

Environment Settings

4   Results and Discussion

4.1   Cross-Validation Results

Our method achieved an average DSC of 0.767 ± 0.032 and NSD of 0.797 ± 0.037 across the 40 hidden test cases of AortaSeg24, placing 5th of 32 teams. We also used an ensemble voting scheme (3-of-5) across independently trained models. Table 6 reports per-region performance on the training set; Fig. 5 shows qualitative results (Table 5).

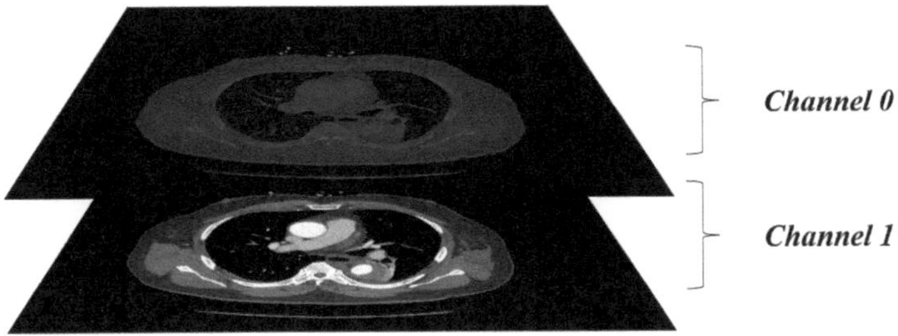

Fig. 4. Two-channel input for segmentation. Channel 0: full HU range $[-1024, 3071]$; Channel 1: soft-tissue window $[-200, 300]$.

Table 3. Training protocol for object detection (YOLOv7).

Pre-trained model	None
Batch size	2
Input size	512×512 (2D)
Total epochs	100
Optimizer	Adam
Initial learning rate	1×10^{-4}
Loss function	Objectness + Class + IoU
Model parameters	$\sim$38M
FLOPs	$\sim$150G

Table 4. Training protocol for segmentation (DynUNet).

Pre-trained model	None
Batch size	2
Patch size	Sec. 1/2: $128 \times 128 \times 112$; Sec. 3: $128 \times 112 \times 160$
Total iterations	200,000
Optimizer	Stochastic gradient descent
Initial learning rate	1×10^{-2}
LR decay schedule	Polynomial decay
Loss function	Dice + Cross-entropy
Training time	$\sim$60 h per model
Model parameters	$\sim$15M
FLOPs	$\sim$90G

Table 5. Development environment.

System	Ubuntu 20.04.5 LTS
CPU	AMD Ryzen 9 7950X (16 cores) @ 4.5 GHz
RAM	128 GB
GPU (type and count)	NVIDIA GeForce RTX 4090 (24 GB)
CUDA version	12.2
Programming language	Python 3.9
Deep learning framework	PyTorch 2.0.0, MONAI 1.3.1

Successful Cases. Performance was strongest for large, well-contrasted vessels with clear boundaries, such as Zone 0, Zone 5, and the external iliac arteries (Fig. 6).

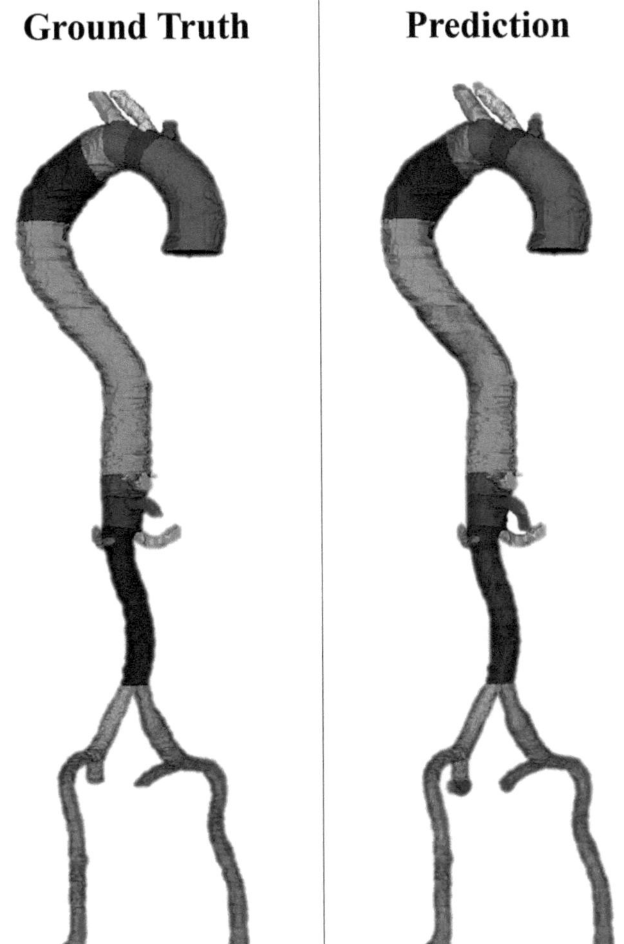

Fig. 5. 3D visualization of ground truth (left) and predictions (right). The overall vascular topology is preserved with fine delineation of major branches.

Challenging Cases and Failure Modes. Zones 1–3 and 6–8 showed relatively lower Dice because labels subdivide a continuous vessel along the superior–inferior axis, introducing semantic ambiguity (Fig. 7). Smaller branches (e.g., celiac, renal) suffered from class imbalance and partial-volume effects.

4.2   Results on Final Testing Set

On the hidden test set (40 scans, 23 labels), our method achieved 0.767 ± 0.032 DSC and 0.797 ± 0.037 NSD, ranking 6th out of 32 teams. Below, Table 7 lists results in a vertical (per-region) layout for readability.

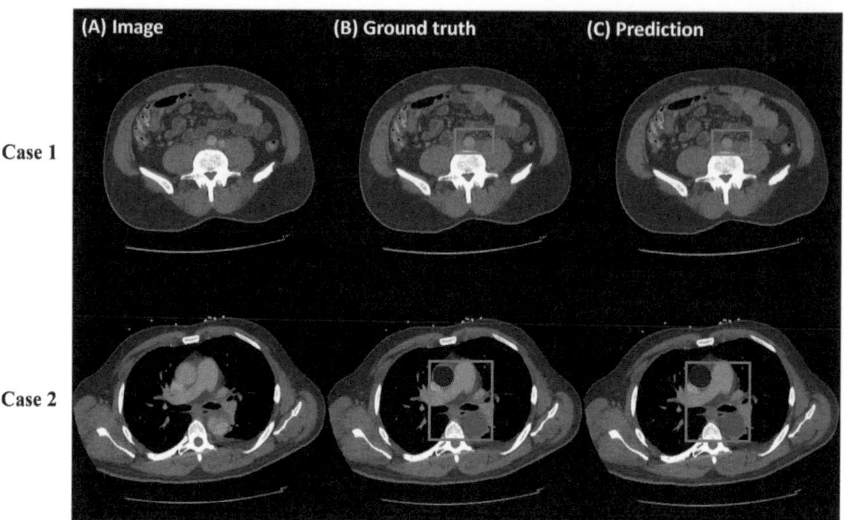

Fig. 6. Successful case. (A) CTA, (B) ground truth, (C) prediction. Renal and iliac arteries show close agreement.

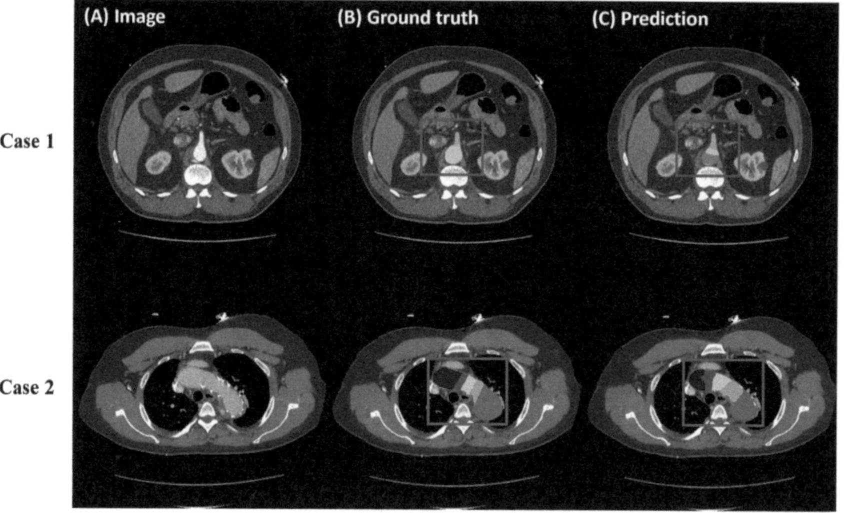

Fig. 7. Challenging case. (A) CTA, (B) ground truth, (C) prediction. Geometric subdivisions of a continuous vessel yield ambiguous boundaries between adjacent zones.

Table 6. Per-region results on the training dataset. Boldface highlights the overall summary row.

Anatomical Region	Avg. DSC	Avg. NSD
Zone 0	0.911 ± 0.009	0.697 ± 0.043
Innominate Artery	0.760 ± 0.043	0.685 ± 0.066
Zone 1	0.640 ± 0.027	0.417 ± 0.023
Left Common Carotid Artery	0.785 ± 0.013	0.815 ± 0.027
Zone 2	0.710 ± 0.021	0.422 ± 0.023
Left Subclavian Artery	0.831 ± 0.015	0.809 ± 0.027
Zone 3	0.700 ± 0.028	0.398 ± 0.042
Zone 4	0.743 ± 0.037	0.476 ± 0.049
Zone 5	0.890 ± 0.016	0.681 ± 0.056
Zone 6	0.721 ± 0.029	0.484 ± 0.037
Celiac Artery	0.677 ± 0.057	0.705 ± 0.061
Zone 7	0.653 ± 0.037	0.482 ± 0.033
Superior Mesenteric Artery	0.718 ± 0.034	0.753 ± 0.037
Zone 8	0.644 ± 0.035	0.484 ± 0.040
Right Renal Artery	0.718 ± 0.045	0.808 ± 0.041
Left Renal Artery	0.636 ± 0.068	0.705 ± 0.079
Zone 9	0.897 ± 0.013	0.780 ± 0.015
Right Common Iliac Artery	0.846 ± 0.017	0.777 ± 0.030
Left Common Iliac Artery	0.866 ± 0.014	0.811 ± 0.025
Right Internal Iliac Artery	0.733 ± 0.037	0.755 ± 0.041
Left Internal Iliac Artery	0.729 ± 0.041	0.739 ± 0.060
Right External Iliac Artery	0.849 ± 0.010	0.864 ± 0.026
Left External Iliac Artery	0.851 ± 0.013	0.870 ± 0.025
Overall	**0.766 ± 0.071**	**0.704 ± 0.106**

Table 7. AortaSeg24 testing results (mean ± std across 40 cases). Rows are grouped per anatomical region with our method above the baseline in each block. *Baseline: CIS-UNet* [5].

Anatomical Region	Method	Avg. DSC	Avg. NSD
Zone 0	Our Method	**0.885 ± 0.076**	**0.785 ± 0.143**
	Baseline	0.880 ± 0.064	0.773 ± 0.119
Innominate	Our Method	**0.766 ± 0.172**	**0.827 ± 0.169**
	Baseline	0.691 ± 0.164	0.739 ± 0.175
Zone 1	Our Method	**0.612 ± 0.151**	0.552 ± 0.134
	Baseline	0.604 ± 0.164	**0.560 ± 0.150**
Left Common Carotid	Our Method	**0.822 ± 0.050**	**0.927 ± 0.052**
	Baseline	0.743 ± 0.108	0.837 ± 0.117
Zone 2	Our Method	**0.693 ± 0.122**	**0.564 ± 0.134**
	Baseline	0.659 ± 0.143	0.543 ± 0.153
Left Subclavian Artery	Our Method	**0.823 ± 0.073**	**0.898 ± 0.087**
	Baseline	0.789 ± 0.115	0.859 ± 0.115
Zone 3	Our Method	**0.689 ± 0.151**	**0.553 ± 0.160**
	Baseline	0.660 ± 0.171	0.517 ± 0.181
Zone 4	Our Method	**0.775 ± 0.105**	**0.654 ± 0.146**
	Baseline	0.746 ± 0.122	0.620 ± 0.139
Zone 5	Our Method	**0.909 ± 0.034**	**0.870 ± 0.067**
	Baseline	0.879 ± 0.054	0.826 ± 0.096
Zone 6	Our Method	0.707 ± 0.186	0.670 ± 0.202
	Baseline	**0.731 ± 0.123**	**0.678 ± 0.164**
Celiac Artery	Our Method	**0.630 ± 0.186**	**0.790 ± 0.178**
	Baseline	0.568 ± 0.178	0.728 ± 0.168
Zone 7	Our Method	0.679 ± 0.150	0.659 ± 0.170
	Baseline	**0.699 ± 0.116**	**0.660 ± 0.146**
SMA	Our Method	**0.723 ± 0.130**	**0.838 ± 0.125**
	Baseline	0.678 ± 0.131	0.782 ± 0.135
Zone 8	Our Method	**0.670 ± 0.160**	**0.678 ± 0.152**
	Baseline	0.664 ± 0.160	0.656 ± 0.160
Right Renal Artery	Our Method	**0.729 ± 0.135**	**0.879 ± 0.142**
	Baseline	0.697 ± 0.142	0.851 ± 0.140
Left Renal Artery	Our Method	**0.664 ± 0.163**	**0.812 ± 0.154**
	Baseline	0.593 ± 0.199	0.742 ± 0.216
Zone 9	Our Method	**0.899 ± 0.063**	**0.887 ± 0.120**
	Baseline	0.879 ± 0.081	0.860 ± 0.130
Right Common Iliac Artery	Our Method	**0.868 ± 0.063**	**0.914 ± 0.091**
	Baseline	0.800 ± 0.132	0.840 ± 0.148
Left Common Iliac Artery	Our Method	**0.841 ± 0.069**	**0.904 ± 0.091**
	Baseline	0.786 ± 0.135	0.842 ± 0.164
Right Internal Iliac Artery	Our Method	**0.776 ± 0.088**	**0.901 ± 0.095**
	Baseline	0.661 ± 0.167	0.773 ± 0.179
Left Internal Iliac Artery	Our Method	**0.727 ± 0.163**	**0.852 ± 0.174**
	Baseline	0.640 ± 0.197	0.767 ± 0.205
Right External Iliac Artery	Our Method	**0.875 ± 0.060**	**0.960 ± 0.053**
	Baseline	0.789 ± 0.134	0.846 ± 0.143
Left External Iliac Artery	Our Method	**0.868 ± 0.058**	**0.955 ± 0.055**
	Baseline	0.783 ± 0.151	0.851 ± 0.160
Overall	Our Method	**0.767 ± 0.032**	**0.797 ± 0.037**
	Baseline	0.723 ± 0.058	0.746 ± 0.067

4.3 Limitation and Future Work

Our detector occasionally under-localized the aortic root and contiguous central segments, leading to suboptimal crops and lower accuracy in Zones 1–3 and 6–8. Future work will explore hybrid localization (detection + attention-based refinement), weak anatomical priors, and multi-planar context to improve robustness for elongated, continuous structures.

5 Conclusion

We presented a two-stage framework combining YOLOv7-based localization with region-wise 3D DynUNets for aortic segmentation in CTA. The method achieves competitive accuracy on AortaSeg24 while remaining memory-efficient, supporting practical deployment for vascular analysis.

Acknowledgments. We thank all data contributors for making the medical images publicly available, and Grand Challenge for hosting the platform. This study was conducted as part of the MICCAI 2024 AortaSeg24 Challenge.

Disclosure of Interests. The authors have no competing interests to declare that are relevant to the content of this article.

Ethical Compliance Statement. All data used was publicly available and anonymized.

References

1. Cardoso, M., et al.: MONAI: an open-source framework for deep learning in healthcare. arXiv preprint arXiv:2211.02701 (2022)
2. Hatamizadeh, A., Nath, V., Tang, Y., Yang, D., Roth, H., Xu, D.: Swin UNETR: swin transformers for semantic segmentation of brain tumors in MRI images. In: International MICCAI Brainlesion Workshop (2021)
3. Hatamizadeh, A., et al.: UNETR: transformers for 3D medical image segmentation. In: Proceedings of the IEEE/CVF Winter Conference on Applications of Computer Vision (2022)
4. Huang, L., et al.: Deep learning techniques for imaging diagnosis and treatment of aortic aneurysm. Front. Cardiovasc. Med. **11**, 1354517 (2024)
5. Imran, M., et al.: CIS-UNet: multi-class segmentation of the aorta in computed tomography angiography via context-aware shifted window self-attention. Comput. Med. Imaging Graph. **118**, 102470 (2024)
6. Imran, M., et al.: Multi-class segmentation of aortic branches and zones in computed tomography angiography: the AortaSeg24 challenge. arXiv preprint arXiv:2502.05330 (2025)
7. Isensee, F., Jaeger, P., Kohl, S., Petersen, J., Maier-Hein, K.: nnU-Net: a self-configuring method for deep learning-based biomedical image segmentation. Nat. Methods **18**(2), 203–211 (2021)
8. Podobnik, G., et al.: HaN-Seg: the head and neck organ-at-risk CT and MR segmentation challenge. Radiother. Oncol. **198**, 110410 (2024)

 9. Roy, S., et al.: MedNeXt: transformer-driven scaling of convnets for medical image segmentation. arXiv preprint arXiv:2303.09975 (2023)
10. Wang, Y., Wang, H., Xin, Z.: Efficient detection model of steel strip surface defects based on YOLO-v7. IEEE Access **10**, 133936–133944 (2022)
11. Wasserthal, J., et al.: TotalSegmentator: robust segmentation of 104 anatomic structures in CT images. Radiol. Artif. Intell. **5**(5) (2023)

Combining Region-Based and Topological Losses in the nnU-Net Framework for Advanced Aorta Segmentation

Markus Tiefenthaler[1]([ORCID]), Enrique Almar-Munoz[1][ORCID], Matthias Schwab[1][ORCID], Elke Ruth Gizewski[1,3][ORCID], Lukas Neumann[2][ORCID], and Stephanie Mangesius[1,3][ORCID]

[1] Department of Radiology, Medical University of Innsbruck, Anichstraße 35, 6020 Innsbruck, Austria
`markus.tiefenthaler@i-med.ac.at`
[2] Department of Engineering Mathematics, University of Innsbruck, Technikerstraße 13, 6020 Innsbruck, Austria
[3] Neuroimaging Research Core Facility, Medical University of Innsbruck, Anichstraße 35, 6020 Innsbruck, Austria

Abstract. Automatic aorta segmentation is important in medical imaging for accurate diagnosis and treatment planning. To allow for minimal invasive repairs for aortic diseases, a detailed 3D analysis of the aortic and branch vessel anatomy is essential. In this study, we propose an enhanced multi-class segmentation approach that combines region-based, voxel-wise, and topological loss functions within the nnU-Net framework. Our method was evaluated on the official test set of the AortaSeg24 challenge, achieving a validation Dice score of 0.752 ± 0.052 and a Normalized Surface Distance (NSD) of 0.782 ± 0.055, representing an improvement over the challenge baseline (Dice: 0.723 ± 0.058, NSD: 0.746 ± 0.067). Due to the challenge's inference time constraints, a trade-off between ensemble size and sliding window step size was required. Experiments showed that using a larger ensemble of networks with an increased sliding window step size yielded better performance than using fewer networks with a smaller step size. The code for inference is available on Github.

Keywords: Aorta · Segmentation · U-Net · Loss functions

1 Introduction

Arterial segmentation, particularly of the aorta, is essential for the diagnosis, risk stratification, and treatment planning of complex vascular diseases [7]. As the body's largest artery, the aorta transports oxygenated blood from the heart to critical organs and tissues. Conditions affecting the aorta and its branches, such as dissection, aneurysms, and atherosclerosis, pose immediate, life-threatening risks, often requiring swift surgical intervention [11].

Advances in medical imaging, like computed tomography angiography (CTA), and therapeutic options, such as endovascular aortic stent grafts, have revolutionized treatment approaches. For instance, minimally invasive repairs of abdominal aortic aneurysms, which are now performed in over 80% of cases, rely

M. Imran et al. (Eds.): AortaSeg 2024, LNCS 16399, pp. 47–58, 2026.
https://doi.org/10.1007/978-3-032-14246-7_5

heavily on precise 3D analysis of the aorta's anatomy [16]. Accurate artery segmentation enables detailed measurements of the aorta's volume and diameter, facilitating optimal device selection and enhancing patient outcomes through tailored, minimally invasive procedures [2].

Despite these advances, automatic, robust segmentation of the aorta and its numerous branches (see Fig. 1) remains a significant technical challenge due to anatomical variability, pathological changes, and limited training data.

Related Work and Motivation. Recent efforts have explored deep learning-based approaches for artery segmentation, achieving notable success in thoracic and abdominal aorta segmentation [4,9]. However, existing methods often focus on the aorta as a single structure, neglecting the clinical significance of its branches and zones, which are critical for endovascular planning and risk prediction.

To address this gap, the AortaSeg24 Challenge [5], organized as part of MICCAI 2024, provides a benchmark for multi-class segmentation of the aorta, including 23 clinically relevant zones and branch vessels. The challenge is based on CTA scans from patients with type B aortic dissection, a high-risk condition requiring precise anatomical understanding for treatment planning. By offering annotated datasets and a unified evaluation framework, AortaSeg promotes the development and comparison of methods that can handle fine-grained anatomical labeling under realistic clinical constraints.

More recently, several methods have emphasized anatomical consistency in artery segmentation [8,15], aiming to ensure that vessel structures are continuous and free from false interruptions caused by the network's predictions. While the risk of discontinuity is relatively low for the main aortic trunk, it remains a concern for smaller branches emerging from the aortic arch, where interruptions can compromise the anatomical plausibility and clinical utility of the segmentation.

Our Contributions. In this work, we investigate the impact of different loss functions within the nnUNet framework [6]. As the official implementation of the SkeletonRecall loss was not publicly available as of July 2024, we re-implemented it based on the description in [8] (see our implementation on Github). We conducted an ablation study to evaluate how various loss functions interact and contribute to segmentation performance. Our final configuration combines Dice loss, TopK loss, and SkeletonRecall, aiming to balance region overlap, hard-to-segment structures, and anatomical continuity. We evaluated our approach on the AortaSeg24 test set, demonstrating improvements over the baseline in both Dice Similarity Coefficient (DSC) and Normalized Surface Distance (NSD) metrics.

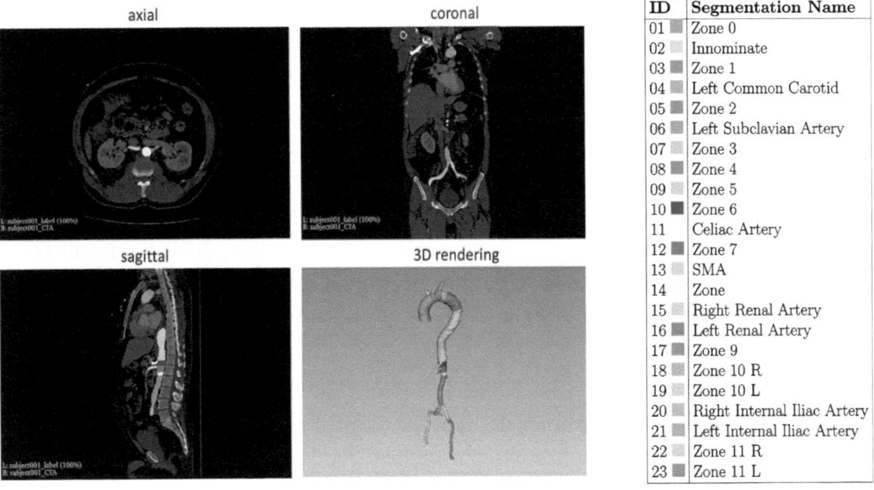

ID	Segmentation Name
01	Zone 0
02	Innominate
03	Zone 1
04	Left Common Carotid
05	Zone 2
06	Left Subclavian Artery
07	Zone 3
08	Zone 4
09	Zone 5
10	Zone 6
11	Celiac Artery
12	Zone 7
13	SMA
14	Zone
15	Right Renal Artery
16	Left Renal Artery
17	Zone 9
18	Zone 10 R
19	Zone 10 L
20	Right Internal Iliac Artery
21	Left Internal Iliac Artery
22	Zone 11 R
23	Zone 11 L

Fig. 1. AortaSeg24 data example with axial, coronal, and sagittal 3D CTA view and 3D rendering of all 23 subclasses of the aortic arch. On the right hand side the names of the different arterial parts are displayed.

2 Method

2.1 Network Architecture: NnUNet

For the AortaSeg24 MICCAI Challenge, we employed the nnUNet framework [6], specifically utilizing the 3D *PlainConvUNet* architecture based on the design introduced in [12]. The network was configured with an initial feature size of 32, expanding across five stages to a maximum of 320 features at the deepest layer. Instance normalization was used throughout with LeakyReLU [10] as the non-linear activation function. Data augmentation followed the default settings provided by the nnUNet framework, with the exception of mirroring, which was disabled.

2.2 Loss Function

The primary contribution of our approach lies in the exploration and implementation of a combination of loss functions to enhance the model's segmentation performance. The final configuration incorporated Dice Loss [3], TopK Loss [17], and Skeleton Recall Loss [8], which together provided synergistic improvements in both volumetric and topological accuracy. Each loss function in our approach addresses a distinct aspect of the segmentation problem [1].

Dice Loss operates at the region level and directly optimizes the overlap between the predicted and ground truth masks, ensuring robust segmentation of underrepresented aortic branches. Its strength lies in effectively handling class imbalance by balancing precision and recall, making it especially suitable for regions where small but crucial anatomical details are present.

Skeleton Recall Loss is particularly valuable in the context of arterial segmentation due to its focus on topological accuracy. Operating at the topology level, this loss function emphasizes the correct delineation of the centerline structures of the aortic branches, which is essential given the complex tubular morphology of these vessels. Compared to centerline Dice Loss (clDice) [13], Skeleton Recall Loss offers a computationally efficient approach that prioritizes connectivity, ensuring that the segmented structures remain anatomically coherent.

TopK Loss operates at the voxel level and is designed to improve model sensitivity to the most challenging and error-prone regions, typically the less-represented or more complex aortic branches. By focusing on the most difficult and weakly predicted voxels, it enhances the model's performance in critical areas where segmentation errors are more likely, helping to capture finer details that are otherwise overlooked [1].

The combination of these loss functions was pivotal in refining the model's ability to accurately segment the aorta. Dice Loss provided a strong foundation for volumetric segmentation, while Skeleton Recall Loss and TopK Loss helped to ensure that both the connectivity of the vascular structures and the precision of finer details were preserved. All loss functions were equally weighted, ensuring that no single objective dominated the training process. This balanced, multi-level loss design allowed the model to manage trade-offs across regional, voxel-level, and topological accuracy, resulting in improved overall performance.

3   Experiments

3.1   Dataset and Evaluation Protocol

We utilized the dataset and evaluation framework provided by the AortaSeg24 Challenge [5], held in conjunction with MICCAI 2024. All data used was publicly available and anonymized. The challenge addresses the task of multi-class segmentation of the aorta and its branches in computed tomography angiography (CTA), encompassing 23 clinically significant aortic branches and zones, see Fig. 1.

The dataset comprises 100 annotated 3D CTA scans from patients diagnosed with uncomplicated type B aortic dissection. Each scan was manually annotated by trained researchers and subsequently reviewed by an experienced vascular surgeon to ensure clinical validity. Annotations include major aortic branches (e.g., renal, iliac, and celiac arteries) as well as SVS/STS zones, following established clinical guidelines. For consistency, all volumes were resampled to an isotropic resolution of $1 \times 1 \times 1\text{mm}^3$.

Out of the 100 scans, 50 were allocated for training, while the remaining 50 were divided into validation and hidden test sets by the challenge organizers. The use of any external data was strictly prohibited during model development.

Further the challenge hosts initiated a time constraint of 5 minutes per patient.

Segmentation performance was assessed using two widely accepted metrics:

1. **Dice Similarity Coefficient (DSC)** – measures the volumetric overlap between predicted and ground-truth segmentations.
2. **Normalized Surface Distance (NSD)** – evaluates boundary accuracy within a tolerance of 2mm

3.2   Implementation Details

Environment Settings. The development environment and software requirements are summarized in Table 1.

Table 1. Development environments and requirements.

System	Ubuntu
CPU	11th Gen Intel(R) Core(TM) i7-11700K
RAM	32GB
GPU (number and type)	One NVIDIA A4000
CUDA version	11.8
Programming language	Python 3.12
Deep learning framework	torch 2.5.1, torchvision 0.2.1

Training Protocols. We opted against utilizing mirroring, as it introduced difficulties in distinguishing between left and right anatomical structures. We trained five folds, each using 40 subjects as training and 10 for validation. Each model was trained for 1000 epochs to ensure comprehensive learning and generalization. For the final submission, we selected the networks weights that achieved the best performance on their respective validation datasets. For further details on the training protocols see Table 2.

Data Preprocessing. To address RAM limitations, we cropped the input volume by 25 voxels on the z-axis and 100 voxels on the x- and y-axes from both sides. Additionally, we implemented a block-wise *softmax* to further manage memory constraints. All input data were preprocessed using Z-score normalization to standardize intensity distributions across samples.

Inference. Throughout the development phase, we explored different strategies to balance segmentation accuracy with the inference time constraint imposed by the AortaSeg challenge. We observed that using larger model ensembles had a more significant positive impact on segmentation performance than reducing the sliding window step size. Based on these findings, our final inference setup consisted of an ensemble of five models with a sliding window step size of 0.4, which provided the best trade-off between prediction quality and runtime compliance.

Table 2. Training protocols.

Pre-trained Model	None
Batch size	2
Patch size	176×112×112
Total epochs	1000
Optimizer	SGD
Initial learning rate (lr)	0.1
Lr decay schedule	PolyLRScheduler
Training time	10 h
Loss function	DSC+TopK+SkeletonRecall
Number of model parameters	31M
Number of flops	552G

4   Results and Discussion

We evaluated our model on both the training dataset of the challenge using 5-fold cross-validation and the hidden test dataset provided by the challenge organizers. The goal was to assess the influence of different loss configurations on segmentation performance across a wide range of anatomical regions, with a focus on both qualitative and quantitative outcomes.

4.1   Evaluation on Training Dataset

We tested the influence of the loss functions using 5 fold cross validation and report the results in Table 3. We trained on 40 subjects and validated on 10. The results are than averaged over all validation subsets for each loss configuration, namely the default Dice loss with Cross Entropy, Dice loss with TopK loss and Dice loss, TopK and SkeletonRecall. While the performance on the different aortic zones are rather close, there is an increase in segmentation accuracy regarding most of the branches. Hinting on a positive effect of the Skeleton Recall loss, especially for the branches.

Figure 2 presents qualitative results for two subjects. The first-row subject achieved high performance. However, challenges remain in segmenting the arterial branches. The models differ in their predicted branch lengths, and some exhibit disconnected segments. Notably, the first subject displays a rare anatomical variant in which two right renal arteries originate from the aortic arch. While the ground truth includes one branch, the models segment the other. Despite this, the first case shows improved branch connectivity of the proposed triple loss configuration compared to the default method.

In contrast, the second subject reveals limitations of the Skeleton Recall loss, since it does not fully prevent the prediction of interrupted arteries, as seen in the segmentation of the left renal artery. Additionally, both cases exhibit a recurring

Table 3. Quantitative evaluation results for the training dataset. The table reports average Dice and NSD scores (mean $\pm$ standard deviation). Best results for each anatomical region are shown in bold.

Anatomical Region	DSC CE Avg. DSC	DSC TopK Avg. DSC	DSC TopK SkelRecall Avg. DSC
Zone 0	0.906 ± 0.028	0.905 ± 0.031	$\mathbf{0.910 \pm 0.030}$
Innominate	0.733 ± 0.138	0.736 ± 0.139	$\mathbf{0.768 \pm 0.117}$
Zone 1	0.671 ± 0.145	$\mathbf{0.678 \pm 0.140}$	0.672 ± 0.147
Left Common Carotid	0.775 ± 0.088	0.775 ± 0.082	$\mathbf{0.797 \pm 0.074}$
Zone 2	0.707 ± 0.104	$\mathbf{0.709 \pm 0.094}$	0.707 ± 0.105
Left Subclavian Artery	0.810 ± 0.061	0.810 ± 0.061	$\mathbf{0.820 \pm 0.069}$
Zone 3	0.703 ± 0.113	0.701 ± 0.110	$\mathbf{0.707 \pm 0.121}$
Zone 4	0.734 ± 0.127	0.733 ± 0.129	$\mathbf{0.793 \pm 0.100}$
Zone 5	0.864 ± 0.059	0.864 ± 0.056	$\mathbf{0.897 \pm 0.053}$
Zone 6	$\mathbf{0.710 \pm 0.122}$	0.709 ± 0.122	0.710 ± 0.131
Celiac Artery	$\mathbf{0.651 \pm 0.175}$	0.648 ± 0.168	0.635 ± 0.200
Zone 7	0.691 ± 0.141	$\mathbf{0.691 \pm 0.137}$	0.681 ± 0.143
SMA	0.678 ± 0.138	0.685 ± 0.132	$\mathbf{0.706 \pm 0.141}$
Zone 8	0.681 ± 0.158	0.680 ± 0.149	$\mathbf{0.681 \pm 0.141}$
Right Renal Artery	0.686 ± 0.175	0.687 ± 0.180	$\mathbf{0.692 \pm 0.156}$
Left Renal Artery	$\mathbf{0.653 \pm 0.147}$	0.628 ± 0.162	0.648 ± 0.161
Zone 9	$\mathbf{0.898 \pm 0.030}$	0.898 ± 0.031	0.897 ± 0.030
Right Common Iliac Artery	0.821 ± 0.105	0.830 ± 0.092	$\mathbf{0.833 \pm 0.094}$
Left Common Iliac Artery	0.849 ± 0.056	0.849 ± 0.045	$\mathbf{0.853 \pm 0.050}$
Right Internal Iliac Artery	$\mathbf{0.698 \pm 0.160}$	0.690 ± 0.161	0.697 ± 0.159
Left Internal Iliac Artery	0.683 ± 0.110	0.665 ± 0.123	$\mathbf{0.720 \pm 0.084}$
Right External Iliac Artery	0.809 ± 0.069	0.812 ± 0.059	$\mathbf{0.831 \pm 0.060}$
Left External Iliac Artery	0.818 ± 0.067	0.813 ± 0.081	$\mathbf{0.844 \pm 0.050}$
Overall	0.749 ± 0.142	0.748 ± 0.142	$\mathbf{0.761 \pm 0.142}$

issue at the boundary between zone 4 and zone 5 for all configurations. Here, model predictions for zone 4 often extend significantly beyond the manually defined region, occasionally including disconnected zone 4 segments within the zone 5 region.

These results illustrate common challenges faced by all methods. Furthermore, we observed inconsistencies in the manual annotations, particularly in the extent to which branching arteries are included (e.g., celiac or left renal artery). Such inconsistencies, found across several subjects and branch types in the public dataset, may introduce ambiguity during training and contribute to decreased segmentation accuracy.

4.2   Results on Test Dataset

Table 4 compares the performance of our framework to the baseline model, CIS-UNet [4], on the hidden test set consisting of 40 subjects. The evaluation was

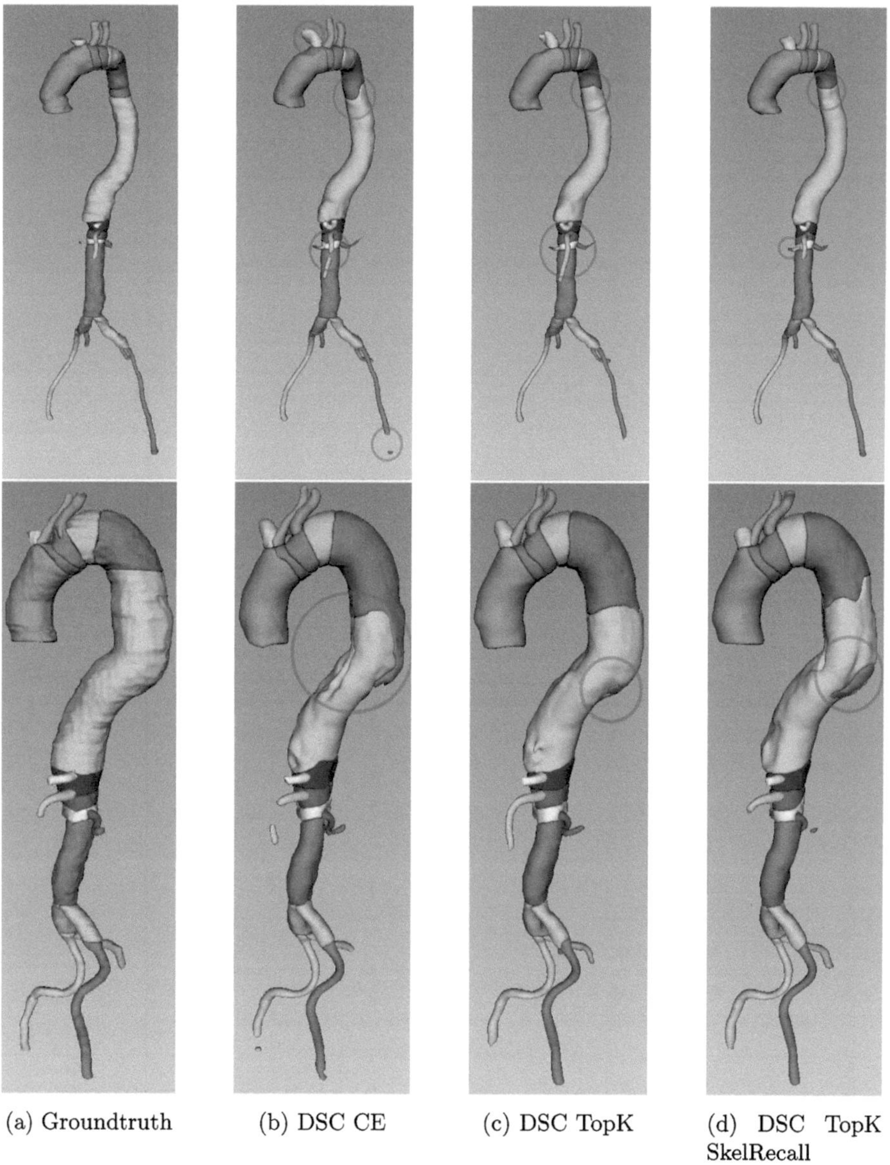

(a) Groundtruth   (b) DSC CE   (c) DSC TopK   (d) DSC TopK SkelRecall

Fig. 2. Qualitative comparison between the ground truth (a) and nnUNet outputs under varying loss configurations (b-d), with red circles indicating regions of consistent model difficulty. (Color figure online)

Table 4. Quantitative evaluation on the AortaSeg24 test dataset. The table reports average Dice and NSD scores (mean ± standard deviation) across all 40 test cases for each anatomical region. Best results for each class and metric are shown in bold.

Anatomical Region	Our Method		Baseline Method [4]	
	Avg. DSC ↑	Avg. NSD ↑	Avg. DSC ↑	Avg. NSD ↑
Zone 0	0.832 ± 0.128	0.720 ± 0.169	**0.880 ± 0.064**	**0.773 ± 0.119**
Innominate	**0.749 ± 0.157**	**0.807 ± 0.156**	0.691 ± 0.164	0.739 ± 0.175
Zone 1	**0.615 ± 0.163**	0.555 ± 0.153	0.604 ± 0.164	**0.560 ± 0.150**
Left Common Carotid	**0.806 ± 0.060**	**0.923 ± 0.052**	0.743 ± 0.108	0.837 ± 0.117
Zone 2	**0.693 ± 0.111**	**0.566 ± 0.148**	0.659 ± 0.143	0.543 ± 0.153
Left Subclavian Artery	**0.822 ± 0.073**	**0.903 ± 0.087**	0.789 ± 0.115	0.859 ± 0.115
Zone 3	**0.695 ± 0.155**	**0.559 ± 0.159**	0.660 ± 0.171	0.517 ± 0.181
Zone 4	**0.784 ± 0.114**	**0.678 ± 0.140**	0.746 ± 0.122	0.620 ± 0.139
Zone 5	0.871 ± 0.099	**0.834 ± 0.121**	**0.879 ± 0.054**	0.826 ± 0.096
Zone 6	0.697 ± 0.118	0.624 ± 0.168	**0.731 ± 0.123**	**0.678 ± 0.164**
Celiac Artery	**0.621 ± 0.179**	**0.794 ± 0.187**	0.568 ± 0.178	0.728 ± 0.168
Zone 7	0.692 ± 0.133	0.647 ± 0.169	**0.699 ± 0.116**	**0.660 ± 0.146**
SMA	**0.694 ± 0.168**	**0.812 ± 0.166**	0.678 ± 0.131	0.782 ± 0.135
Zone 8	**0.685 ± 0.120**	**0.669 ± 0.138**	0.664 ± 0.160	0.656 ± 0.160
Right Renal Artery	**0.710 ± 0.163**	**0.878 ± 0.183**	0.697 ± 0.142	0.851 ± 0.140
Left Renal Artery	**0.662 ± 0.154**	**0.820 ± 0.163**	0.593 ± 0.199	0.742 ± 0.216
Zone 9	**0.886 ± 0.124**	**0.871 ± 0.165**	0.879 ± 0.081	0.860 ± 0.130
Right Common Iliac Artery	**0.847 ± 0.121**	**0.896 ± 0.125**	0.800 ± 0.132	0.840 ± 0.148
Left Common Iliac Artery	**0.861 ± 0.048**	**0.922 ± 0.074**	0.786 ± 0.135	0.842 ± 0.164
Right Internal Iliac Artery	**0.744 ± 0.154**	**0.881 ± 0.147**	0.661 ± 0.167	0.773 ± 0.179
Left Internal Iliac Artery	**0.710 ± 0.162**	**0.837 ± 0.174**	0.640 ± 0.197	0.767 ± 0.205
Right External Iliac Artery	**0.808 ± 0.172**	**0.899 ± 0.158**	0.789 ± 0.134	0.846 ± 0.143
Left External Iliac Artery	**0.802 ± 0.138**	**0.885 ± 0.134**	0.783 ± 0.151	0.851 ± 0.160
Overall	**0.752 ± 0.052**	**0.782 ± 0.055**	0.723 ± 0.058	0.746 ± 0.067

conducted by the challenge organizers, who reported the average DSC and NSD for both methods. Our approach, which incorporates the proposed triple loss function, achieved overall performance improvements, with increases of 0.029 in DSC and 0.036 in NSD compared to the baseline. Although the baseline performed better in a few regions (Zones 0, 5, 6, and 7), our method demonstrated clear advantages in accurately segmenting the aortic branches.

4.3   Limitations

While the presented approach achieved competitive performance, several limitations should be acknowledged.

First, the manual segmentations used for training and evaluation exhibited some inconsistencies, particularly in the inclusion and extent of arterial branches.

Future work could explore strategies to handle label uncertainty or use a clear medical and geometrical end of the branches for the manual annotations.

Second, the handling of rare anatomical variations remains a challenge. Beyond the issue with double right renal arteries, the networks also struggled with other uncommon anatomies. These variations often caused inconsistent segmentation near aortic branching zones, requiring anatomical priors or rule-based postprocessing to ensure plausibility across diverse vascular morphologies.

Third, while the Skeleton Recall loss is effective in promoting connectivity along vascular branches, it may also introduce undesirable centerline artifacts. In particular, the skeletonization algorithm struggles to produce consistent centerline outputs in narrow anatomical regions or where voxel labels are inconsistent. This can result in cone-like artifacts near segment transition as shown in Fig. 3).

To mitigate this, we experimented with restricting the Skeleton Recall loss to branch regions only, applying a sigmoid ramp-up schedule during training to gradually increase its influence. This aimed to enhance branch connectivity while minimizing side effects in non-branch regions. Although conceptually promising, preliminary results obtained using the official Skeleton Recall code showed performance comparable to default nnUNet and nnUNet with DSC TopK loss.

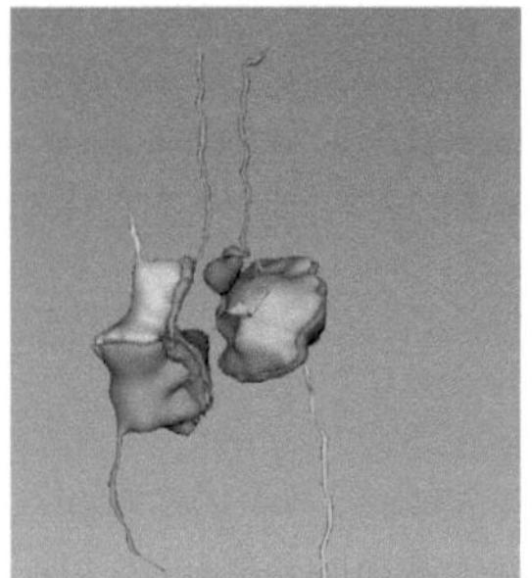  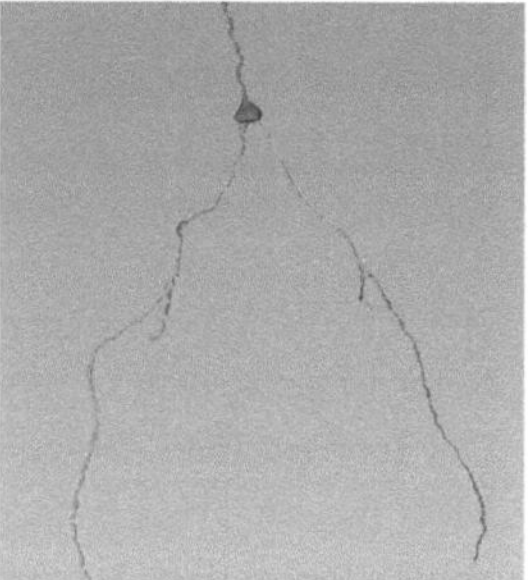

Fig. 3. Example skeleton of the aortic arch and its branches. Cone-like artifacts appear at the boundaries between adjacent segments due to the skeletonization process. The left image shows the top part of the aortic arch, while the right image depicts the bottom part.

4.4   Future Work

Future work will explore unsupervised methods for differentiating between lumen, calcification, and dissection within the aortic and branching arterial structures. This distinction is clinically relevant, particularly in cases of vascular disease where calcified plaques or dissections may interfere with both diagnosis and automated segmentation. We investigated the differentiation between lumen and calcification in the head and neck arteries, beginning at the aortic arch and extending through Zones 0 to 3, up to the Circle of Willis. The results of this study were accepted at the SWITCH 2025 MICCAI workshop [14], demonstrating the feasibility of learning both structural and intensity-based features in an unsupervised setting. Building upon this foundation, future efforts will aim to generalize the approach across the entire aortic arch and incorporate dissection features, with the goal of developing a more anatomically and pathologically informed segmentation pipeline.

5   Conclusion

In this work, we used an extension to the nnUNet framework for automatic segmentation of the aorta and its branches, focusing on improving the delineation of branching structures using a combination of Dice, TopK, and Skeleton Recall loss functions. Our method was evaluated both on a hidden test set provided by the challenge organizers and through five-fold cross-validation on the training data. Quantitative results demonstrate that the proposed triple-loss configuration outperforms the CIS-UNet baseline in overall performance, achieving improvements of 0.029 in DSC and 0.036 in NSD. Notably, our method shows consistent gains in segmenting aortic branches, which are among the most structurally complex and variable regions. Qualitative analysis confirms that integrating Skeleton Recall loss leads to more anatomically plausible and connected segmentations in many challenging cases, compared to models relying on loss configurations without Skeleton Recall loss. Analyzing the skeletonization process, however, shows that artifacts, such as cone-like shapes, occur at boundaries, indicating room for refinement for the skeletonization algorithm. Ensemble strategies further improved performance, with a five-model ensemble proving more effective than simply reducing the step size.

Acknowledgements. We thank all data contributors for making the medical images publicly available, and GrandChallenge for providing the challenge platform. This study was supported by FWF doc.funds (DOC 110) and conducted as part of the MICCAI 2024 AortaSeg24 Challenge.

Disclosure of Interests. The authors have no competing interests to declare that are relevant to the content of this article.

Ethical Compliance Statement. All data used was publicly available and anonymized.

References

1. Azad, R., et al.: Loss functions in the era of semantic segmentation: a survey and outlook arXiv:2312.05391 (2023)
2. Berretta, P., et al.: Minimally invasive approach: is this the future of aortic surgery? Indian J. Thoracic Cardiovasc. Surg. **38**(1), 171–182 (2021). https://doi.org/10.1007/s12055-021-01258-2

3. Dice, L.R.: Measures of the amount of ecologic association between species. Ecology **26**(3), 297–302 (1945). https://doi.org/10.2307/1932409
4. Imran, M., et al.: CIS-UNet: multi-class segmentation of the aorta in computed tomography angiography via context-aware shifted window self-attention. Comput. Med. Imaging Graph. **118**, 102470 (2024). https://doi.org/10.1016/j.compmedimag.2024.102470
5. Imran, M., et al.: Multi-class segmentation of aortic branches and zones in computed tomography angiography: the aortaseg24 challenge (2025). arXiv preprint arXiv:2502.05330
6. Isensee, F., Jaeger, P.F., Kohl, S.A.A., Petersen, J., Maier-Hein, K.H.: nnU-Net: a self-configuring method for deep learning-based biomedical image segmentation. Nat. Methods **18**(2), 203–211 (2021). https://doi.org/10.1038/s41592-020-01008-z
7. Jin, Y., et al.: AI-based aortic vessel tree segmentation for cardiovascular diseases treatment: status quo (2021). arXiv preprint arXiv:2108.02998
8. Kirchhoff, Y., et al.: Skeleton recall loss for connectivity conserving and resource efficient segmentation of thin tubular structures. In: Leonardis, A., Ricci, E., Roth, S., Russakovsky, O., Sattler, T., Varol, G. (eds.) Computer Vision – ECCV 2024, pp. 218–234. Springer Nature Switzerland, Cham (2024) https://doi.org/10.1007/978-3-031-72980-5_13
9. Krebs, J.R., et al.: Volumetric analysis of acute uncomplicated type b aortic dissection using an automated deep learning aortic zone segmentation model. J. Vasc. Surg. **80**(4), 1025–1034 (2024). https://doi.org/10.1016/j.jvs.2024.06.001
10. Maas, A.L., Hannun, A.Y., Ng, A.Y.: Rectifier nonlinearities improve neural network acoustic models. In: Proceedings of the 30th International Conference on Machine Learning, vol. 28 (2013). https://api.semanticscholar.org/CorpusID:16489696
11. Nienaber, C.A., Powell, J.T.: Management of acute aortic syndromes. Eur. Heart J. **33**(1), 26–35 (2012). https://doi.org/10.1093/eurheartj/ehr186
12. Ronneberger, O., Fischer, P., Brox, T.: U-Net: convolutional networks for biomedical image segmentation. In: Navab, N., Hornegger, J., Wells, W.M., Frangi, A.F. (eds.) MICCAI 2015. LNCS, vol. 9351, pp. 234–241. Springer, Cham (2015). https://doi.org/10.1007/978-3-319-24574-4_28
13. Shit, S., et al.: clDice - a novel topology-preserving loss function for tubular structure segmentation. In: 2021 IEEE/CVF Conference on Computer Vision and Pattern Recognition (CVPR), pp. 16555–16564 (2021). https://doi.org/10.1109/CVPR46437.2021.01629
14. Tiefenthaler, M., Deisl, P., Neumann, L., Knoflach, M., Mangesius, S., Gizewski, E.R.: In: From thresholds to teachers: correcting unsupervised learning for arterial calcifications in CTA, pp. 42–51. Springer Nature Switzerland, Cham (2026). https://doi.org/10.1007/978-3-032-07945-9_5
15. Tiefenthaler, M., Mangesius, S., Pereverzyev, S., Gizewski, E.R., Neumann, L.: Shape-aware inference scheme for selective extraction of head-neck arteries on computer tomography angiography images. Comput. Methods Programs Biomed., 108952 (2025). https://doi.org/10.1016/j.cmpb.2025.108952
16. Ultee, K.H., Soden, P.A., Zettervall, S.L., Darling, J., Verhagen, H.J., Schermerhorn, M.L.: Conversion from endovascular to open abdominal aortic aneurysm repair. J. Vasc. Surg. **64**(1), 76–82 (2016). https://doi.org/10.1016/j.jvs.2015.12.055
17. Wu, Z., Shen, C., van den Hengel, A.: Bridging category-level and instance-level semantic image segmentation arXiv:1605.06885 (2016)

Data-Centric Multiclass Aortic Segmentation: Revisiting Classical Architectures in Low-Data Regimes

Marek Wodzinski[1,2(✉)] and Henning Müller[2,3]

[1] Department of Measurement and Electronics, AGH University of Krakow, Krakow, Poland
wodzinski@agh.edu.pl

[2] Information Systems Institute, University of Applied Sciences Western Switzerland (HES-SO Valais-Wallis), Sierre, Switzerland

[3] Medical Faculty, University of Geneva, Geneva, Switzerland

Abstract. This paper presents our submission to the AortaSeg Challenge at MICCAI 2024, which focuses on multiclass segmentation of the aorta into anatomically defined zones and branches. We adopted a data-centric strategy, emphasizing rigorous data preparation and carefully designed pre- and post-processing steps over architectural novelty. Our approach is built upon a classical 3D RUNet-based model, demonstrating that such architectures remain highly competitive in low-data scenarios when paired with robust engineering practices. Specifically, we implemented a two-step, patch-based segmentation pipeline, incorporating targeted data augmentation and class-aware sampling during training. This design aimed to improve performance on small and underrepresented anatomical structures. On the official test dataset, our method achieved an average Dice Similarity Coefficient of 0.755 $\pm$ 0.038 and a Normalized Surface Distance of 0.788 $\pm$ 0.042, outperforming the baseline in the majority of evaluated regions. These results highlight the effectiveness of prioritizing data quality and processing techniques, and underscore the continued relevance of classical segmentation models in practical, data-constrained medical imaging tasks.

Keywords: AortaSeg · Image Segmentation · Aorta · MICCAI · Challenge

1 Introduction

Accurate segmentation of the aorta and its branches is a critical task in cardiovascular image analysis, with direct implications for diagnosis, treatment planning, and surgical navigation. The aorta is a complex anatomical structure, and its segmentation into zones and branches enables more precise localization of pathologies and facilitates standardized reporting. Recent advances in volumetric imaging and deep learning have significantly improved segmentation performance, yet challenges remain, particularly in delineating small or ambiguous anatomical regions [10].

M. Imran et al. (Eds.): AortaSeg 2024, LNCS 16399, pp. 59–73, 2026.
https://doi.org/10.1007/978-3-032-14246-7_6

To address these challenges, the AortaSeg challenge was introduced as part of the MICCAI 2024 conference [8]. The goal of the challenge was to promote the development of robust and generalizable methods for multiclass segmentation of the aorta, including both its zones and major branches. The challenge provides a standardized dataset and evaluation framework, encouraging fair comparison and reproducibility across different approaches.

The task of 3D aortic segmentation has been extensively studied in recent years, driven by the clinical need for accurate anatomical modeling and the availability of large-scale annotated datasets. Traditional approaches relied on atlas-based registration or level-set methods, which, while interpretable, often struggled with anatomical variability and imaging artifacts [11].

With the growing adoption of deep learning, convolutional neural networks (CNNs) have become the dominant paradigm for medical image segmentation. Among these, nnUNet has emerged as a widely adopted, self-configuring framework that adapts its architecture, training, and preprocessing pipelines to a given dataset without manual tuning [9]. Its robustness and generalizability have made it a de facto standard in medical image segmentation benchmarks. Majority of the AortaSeg challenge participants used nnUNet as the baseline for further development.

Vagenas et al. [15], who emphasize the trade-offs between model complexity, data availability, and generalization, provide a broader review of deep learning techniques for 3D volumetric segmentation in biomedical imaging. Their findings support the notion that architectural sophistication alone does not guarantee superior performance, especially in low-data regimes.

The SEG.A 2023 challenge [1], held in conjunction with MICCAI 2023, further highlighted the importance of robust and generalizable segmentation methods. Several top-performing solutions in that challenge employed data-centric strategies, heavy augmentation, and high-resolution models to improve performance on small and ambiguous structures [2,12,16]. Nevertheless, while SEG.A focused on segmenting the aorta as a single anatomical structure, AortaSeg extended this task to a more complex, multi-class segmentation of distinct aortic regions.

Other notable contributions, specific to the aorta segmentation, include multi-view CNN approaches, such as the method by Fantazzini et al. [3], which combines axial, sagittal, and coronal views to improve spatial coherence in aortic lumen segmentation. Their pipeline achieved high Dice scores and demonstrated robustness across different anatomical regions. It is also worth to mentioned the CIS-UNet [7], which integrates convolutional and attention-based modules to capture both local and global contextual information. CIS-UNet was proposed as the baseline for the AortaSeg challenge and has demonstrated strong performance in segmenting complex vascular structures.

Despite these advances, many existing methods still prioritize architectural novelty over data quality and preprocessing strategies. This gap motivates our work, which revisits classical architectures through a data-centric perspective to achieve competitive performance with reduced complexity.

Contribution: In this work, we adopt a data-centric perspective to tackle the problem of multiclass aortic segmentation. Rather than relying on the latest architectural trends, we focus on optimizing the data pipeline that emphasizes careful data preparation, augmentation, and postprocessing. Our experiments reveal that classical architectures, such as RUNet, can outperform more recent models when paired with a robust data-centric strategy, particularly in low-data regimes.

Our key contributions are as follows:

- We propose a data-centric pipeline for multiclass aortic segmentation, prioritizing preprocessing and postprocessing over architectural complexity.
- We demonstrate that a classical RUNet-based model, when properly tuned, achieves state-of-the-art performance on the AortaSeg test set.
- We show that decisions such as two-step segmentation procedure, using as large patch resolution as possible, or adding class weights for patch sampling, impact the segmentation more than using more advanced segmentation architectures, especially in low-data regimes.

2   Method

We propose a two-stage, patch-based segmentation pipeline designed to perform robust multiclass aortic segmentation. The method first segments the entire aorta as a binary structure and then refines this output into anatomically meaningful classes. This design enforces spatial continuity and anatomical consistency across segmented regions. An overview of the pipeline is illustrated in Fig. 1.

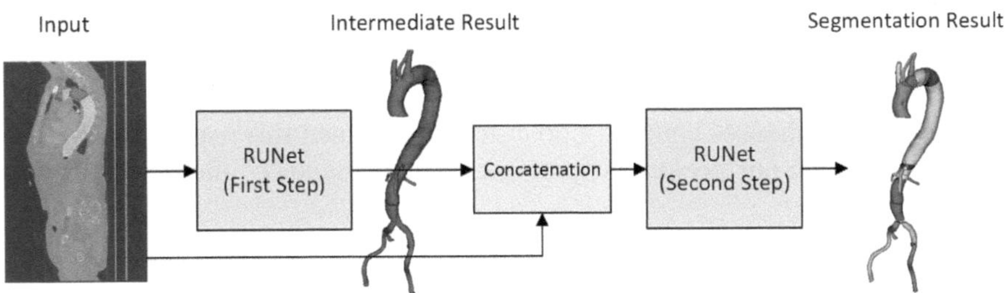

Fig. 1. Visualization of the double-step segmentation pipeline. The processing starts with first segmentation network dedicated to segmenting the whole aorta as a binary structure. The initial segmentation result is concatenated with the CT volume and passed to the second segmentation network devoted to the multiclass segmentation. As a result, the second network does not need to localize the aorta but learn how to distinguish between the aortic branches.

2.1   Network Architecture

Our pipeline consists of two sequential 3D ResUNet models. The first model performs binary segmentation of the aorta, while the second model takes the original image concatenated with the soft binary mask as input to produce the final multiclass segmentation. This two-step design ensures that the multiclass output remains spatially coherent and anatomically plausible.

The encoder in both ResUNet models follows a standard convolutional downsampling path with residual connections. It extracts hierarchical features at multiple scales, which are critical for capturing both global context and fine anatomical details.

The decoder mirrors the encoder with upsampling layers and skip connections, enabling precise localization. The final layer outputs either a binary mask (first model) or a multiclass probability map (second model), followed by an argmax operation during inference.

2.2   Pre-processing

Input CT volumes are split into overlapping 3D patches of size $256 \times 256 \times 256$ for binary segmentation. For the second stage, the binary activation map is concatenated with the original image, and the resulting volume is split into $192 \times 192 \times 192$ patches. Different patch sizes for both stages were selected due to GPU memory constraints; in the second segmentation step the final output has the number of channels equal to the number of aortic zones, significantly increasing the GPU memory required both during training and inference. All patches are normalized and processed independently.

2.3   Objective Function

We use a compound loss function combining Generalized Dice Loss and Focal Loss, both implemented via the MONAI library. This combination balances class imbalance and enhances boundary precision. We defined this particular objective function based on our previous experiences with imbalanced multiclass segmentation.

2.4   Post-processing

Post-processing involves stitching the predicted patches back into the full volume using weighted averaging in overlapping regions. The final multiclass label map is obtained by applying the argmax operator to the softmax output of the second model.

2.5   Augmentation

To enhance model generalization and robustness, we employed an extensive data augmentation pipeline using the TorchIO library [14]. Each training sample underwent intensity normalization followed by a sequence of seven randomly selected transformations from a diverse pool. These included random motion artifacts, gamma correction, affine transformations, axis flipping, anisotropic downsampling, Gaussian noise, and blurring—each applied with a probability of 0.5. Additionally, class imbalance was addressed by applying empirically tuned class weights during training, with higher weights assigned to smaller or more challenging structures (e.g., renal and iliac arteries), thereby improving segmentation performance across underrepresented regions.

2.6   Inference Optimization

To handle large 3D volumes, we used a patch-based strategy with $32 \times 32 \times 32$ overlap between patches to ensure smooth transitions and reduce boundary artifacts.

Due to the 5-min inference time constraint predefined by the Challenge organizers (including Docker loading), we limited the number of folds to two for both segmentation stages. This decision significantly reduced Docker image size and loading time, which accounted for approximately 70% of the total runtime. The actual model inference time averaged around 50 s.

3   Experiments

3.1   Dataset and Evaluation Protocol

We utilized the dataset and evaluation framework provided by the AortaSeg24 Challenge [8], held as part of MICCAI 2024. The challenge centers on the multiclass segmentation of the aorta in computed tomography angiography (CTA), encompassing 23 clinically significant zones and branches. The dataset comprises 100 annotated 3D CTA scans from patients diagnosed with uncomplicated type B aortic dissection. Each scan was manually labeled by trained annotators and subsequently reviewed by a vascular surgery expert to ensure clinical validity. The annotations include major aortic branches—such as the renal, iliac, and celiac arteries—as well as SVS/STS zones, following established clinical standards. All volumes were resampled to a uniform isotropic resolution of $1 \times 1 \times 1$ mm^3 to ensure consistency across samples.

Out of the 100 scans, 50 were allocated for training. The remaining scans were divided into validation and hidden test sets by the challenge organizers. The use of external datasets during model development was strictly prohibited. Only the 50 training cases were available to the challenge participants.

Segmentation performance was assessed using two widely accepted metrics:

1. **Dice Similarity Coefficient (DSC)** – measures volumetric overlap between predicted and ground truth segmentations.
2. **Normalized Surface Distance (NSD)** – evaluates boundary accuracy within a 2 mm tolerance.

3.2 Ablation Studies

To comprehensively evaluate the design choices in AortaSeg, we conducted a series of ablation studies focusing on model architecture, training strategy, data augmentation, input resolution, and sampling techniques. The following experiments were performed:

1. **Comparison with Alternative Architectures**
   We benchmarked our 3D ResUNet against several state-of-the-art segmentation models in a single-step setting, including SwinUNETR [5], UNETR [6], AttentionUNet [13], and SegMamba [4]. This comparison highlights the effectiveness of our chosen architecture in capturing complex aortic structures.
2. **Single-Step vs. Two-Step Segmentation**
   To assess the benefit of our two-step segmentation pipeline, we compared the performance of the 3D ResUNet in both single-step and two-step configurations. The two-step approach, which refines the segmentation in a focused region of interest, demonstrated improved accuracy and boundary delineation.
3. **Impact of Proposed Augmentation Strategy**
   We evaluated the influence of our tailored augmentation pipeline by applying it to both stages of the two-step segmentation. The results show that consistent augmentation across both steps enhances generalization and robustness, particularly in challenging anatomical regions.
4. **Patch Size for Second-Step Segmentation**
   We investigated the effect of input resolution by comparing patch sizes of $128 \times 128 \times 128$ and $192 \times 192 \times 192$ in the second-step segmentation using the 3D ResUNet with augmentation. Larger patches provided more contextual information, leading to improved segmentation performance.
5. **Effect of Class Sampling in Second-Step Segmentation**
   Finally, we examined the role of class-balanced sampling during the second-step training phase. Using the 3D augmented ResUNet with $192 \times 192 \times 192$ patches, we found that class sampling significantly improved the segmentation of underrepresented structures, contributing to more balanced performance across classes.

3.3 Implementation Details

Data Preprocessing. During training, each volume was intensity-normalized to [0–1] range to standardize input distributions. For the binary segmentation stage, volumes were divided into overlapping 3D patches of size $256 \times 256 \times 256$. For the second-stage multiclass segmentation, the original image was concatenated with the soft binary mask (resulting from the first step) and split into $192 \times 192 \times 192$ patches.

During inference, to efficiently handle large-scale 3D data, we employed a patch-based processing strategy with $32 \times 32 \times 32$ overlap between adjacent patches. This overlap mitigated boundary artifacts during inference and enabled smooth reconstruction of the full-volume predictions. Data loading and augmentation were parallelized using the TorchIO library [14], which allowed for efficient on-the-fly transformations and minimized I/O bottlenecks during training. The source code is available in the related GitHub repository [17].

Environment Settings. All experiments were conducted using the Helios high-performance computing cluster provided by the PLGrid infrastructure (ACK Cyfronet AGH), with jobs enqueued in parallel using the hardware configuration detailed in Table 1.

Table 1. Development environments and requirements. Please note that the processing pipeline required relatively large CPU/RAM resources compared to GPU due to the performed data augmentation and sampling.

System	CrayOS (SLES 15sp5)
CPU	288 cores, aarch64 (Helios)
RAM	256 GB
GPU (number and type)	1x NVIDIA GH200 96G
CUDA version	11.8
Programming language	Python 3.10
Libraries	Torch 2.0, TorchIO, MONAI

Training Protocols Data Augmentation: To enhance model generalization and robustness, we employed a comprehensive 3D data augmentation pipeline during training. The augmentations included:

- Spatial transformations: random affine transformations, and flipping along all three axes.
- Intensity transformations: Gaussian noise addition, Gaussian blur, gamma correction, anisotropic downsampling, and random motion artifacts.

In the two-step segmentation setting, augmentations were applied independently to both stages, ensuring diversity in both coarse and refined segmentation inputs. For the second-step, only spatial transformations were applied to the initial segmentation mask.

Data Sampling Strategy: We adopted a class-aware sampling strategy to address class imbalance, particularly in the second-step segmentation. During training, patches were sampled with increased probability from regions containing underrepresented classes (e.g., small or thin anatomical structures). The sampling probability for each class was manually predefined and represented in the sampling table. The exact probabilities are available in the associated repository. This approach ensured that the model received sufficient examples of all classes, improving segmentation consistency and reducing bias toward dominant regions.

Optimal Model Selection Criteria: Model selection was based on performance on a held-out validation set. We monitored the Dice Similarity Coefficient (DSC) for each class and the average DSC across all classes. All folds were trained until convergence and the last checkpoint was used for the evaluation (Tables 2 and 3).

Table 2. Training protocols for the first-step model.

Batch size	1 (16)
Patch size	$256 \times 256 \times 256$
Total epochs	200
Optimizer	AdamW
Initial learning rate (lr)	0.001
Lr decay schedule	Exponential (0.995)
Training time	48 h
Loss function	Generalized Dice Loss + Focal Loss
Number of model parameters	120,738,065
Number of flops	1829.09 G

Table 3. Training protocols for the second-step (and the single-step) model.

Batch size	1 (16)
Patch size	$192 \times 192 \times 192$
Total epochs	200
Optimizer	AdamW
Initial learning rate (lr)	0.001
Lr decay schedule	Exponential (0.995)
Training time	48 h
Loss function	Generalized Dice Loss + Focal Loss
Number of model parameters	120,835,576
Number of flops	2183.69 G

4   Results and Discussion

Our experiments (Table 4) demonstrated that the 3D ResUNet consistently outperformed more recent and complex architectures such as SwinUNETR,

UNETR, AttentionUNet, and SegMamba in the single-step segmentation setting. Despite the growing popularity of transformer-based and hybrid models, these architectures did not yield performance gains in our task. This suggests that for anatomically constrained problems with limited training data, well-optimized convolutional architectures like ResUNet remain highly effective. The lack of improvement from transformer-based models may be attributed to their higher data requirements and sensitivity to hyperparameter tuning, which can be challenging in medical imaging scenarios with limited annotated data.

Table 4. Quantitative comparison of different encoder-decoder architectures on the internal validation set (single step, $192 \times 192 \times 192$), without augmentation and additional sampling. The table reports average DSC and NSD scores (mean $\pm$ standard deviation) aggregated for all training cases using 5-fold cross-validation. Note that the choice of deep network architecture is not crucial for correct multiclass aorta segmentation in the low-data regime and the simplest architecture performs best.

Anatomical Region	ResUNet		SwinUNETR [5]		UNETR [6]		AttentionUNet [13]		SegMamba [4]	
	DSC $\uparrow$	NSD $\uparrow$	DSC $\uparrow$	NSD $\uparrow$	DSC $\uparrow$	NSD $\uparrow$	DSC $\uparrow$	NSD $\uparrow$	DSC $\uparrow$	NSD $\uparrow$
Zone 0	**0.842 ± 0.072**	**0.758 ± 0.115**	0.829 ± 0.082	0.742 ± 0.121	0.741 ± 0.069	0.682 ± 0.103	0.834 ± 0.071	0.724 ± 0.105	0.798 ± 0.074	0.721 ± 0.111
Innominate	**0.671 ± 0.168**	**0.725 ± 0.182**	0.655 ± 0.165	0.707 ± 0.194	0.621 ± 0.134	0.671 ± 0.164	0.665 ± 0.165	0.717 ± 0.192	0.649 ± 0.171	0.698 ± 0.204
Zone 1	0.539 ± 0.154	0.495 ± 0.161	0.498 ± 0.124	0.487 ± 0.154	0.471 ± 0.098	0.455 ± 0.107	**0.541 ± 0.155**	**0.498 ± 0.164**	0.501 ± 0.135	0.491 ± 0.167
Left Common Carotid	**0.707 ± 0.128**	**0.819 ± 0.124**	0.681 ± 0.131	0.793 ± 0.132	0.641 ± 0.089	0.743 ± 0.085	0.701 ± 0.134	0.812 ± 0.135	0.684 ± 0.121	0.796 ± 0.131
Zone 2	**0.623 ± 0.133**	0.521 ± 0.164	0.598 ± 0.138	0.507 ± 0.172	0.552 ± 0.091	0.487 ± 0.128	0.617 ± 0.138	**0.522 ± 0.171**	0.601 ± 0.135	0.509 ± 0.169
Left Subclavian Artery	0.731 ± 0.072	0.831 ± 0.098	0.712 ± 0.081	0.805 ± 0.095	0.655 ± 0.056	0.741 ± 0.071	**0.733 ± 0.074**	**0.834 ± 0.101**	0.715 ± 0.071	0.806 ± 0.091
Zone 3	**0.615 ± 0.158**	0.496 ± 0.152	0.592 ± 0.141	0.487 ± 0.141	0.559 ± 0.108	0.459 ± 0.119	0.613 ± 0.155	**0.498 ± 0.159**	0.594 ± 0.148	0.491 ±0.156
Zone 4	0.729 ± 0.115	0.607 ± 0.131	0.715 ± 0.104	0.594 ± 0.127	0.661 ± 0.089	0.547 ± 0.103	**0.731 ± 0.117**	**0.611 ± 0.139**	0.707 ± 0.101	0.596 ± 0.125
Zone 5	**0.854 ± 0.041**	**0.815 ± 0.088**	0.829 ± 0.039	0.782 ± 0.079	0.781 ± 0.031	0.739 ± 0.064	0.849 ± 0.043	0.813 ± 0.089	0.832 ± 0.041	0.784 ± 0.081
Zone 6	**0.639 ± 0.145**	**0.581 ± 0.181**	0.621 ± 0.132	0.569 ± 0.186	0.574 ± 0.091	0.519 ± 0.129	0.637 ± 0.141	0.580 ± 0.179	0.614 ± 0.139	0.564 ± 0.178
Celiac Artery	0.523 ± 0.148	0.646 ± 0.161	0.514 ± 0.128	0.629 ± 0.173	0.481 ± 0.098	0.571 ± 0.117	**0.531 ± 0.145**	**0.661 ± 0.159**	0.501 ± 0.135	0.623 ± 0.177
Zone 7	**0.614 ± 0.145**	**0.572 ± 0.171**	0.599 ± 0.137	0.554 ± 0.184	0.532 ± 0.107	0.494 ± 0.141	0.607 ± 0.151	0.571 ± 0.184	0.601 ± 0.143	0.568 ± 0.171
SMA	**0.592 ± 0.171**	**0.715 ± 0.178**	0.584 ± 0.182	0.698 ± 0.193	0.514 ± 0.135	0.658 ± 0.125	0.591 ± 0.168	0.707 ± 0.175	0.581 ± 0.174	0.701 ± 0.183
Zone 8	0.642 ±0.128	**0.635 ± 0.165**	0.629 ± 0.145	0.621 ± 0.177	0.584 ± 0.094	0.574 ± 0.134	**0.643 ± 0.137**	0.631 ± 0.173	0.625 ± 0.141	0.622 ± 0.174
Right Renal Artery	**0.623 ± 0.152**	**0.785 ± 0.168**	0.614 ± 0.141	0.769 ± 0.159	0.571 ± 0.113	0.681 ± 0.119	0.619 ± 0.157	0.779 ± 0.173	0.605 ± 0.145	0.768 ± 0.161
Left Renal Artery	0.576 ± 0.167	0.702 ± 0.198	0.568 ± 0.154	0.699 ± 0.174	0.511 ± 0.117	0.646 ± 0.141	**0.583 ± 0.172**	**0.705 ± 0.205**	0.571 ± 0.159	0.701 ± 0.187
Zone 9	**0.852 ± 0.091**	0.842 ± 0.139	0.839 ± 0.094	0.831 ± 0.145	0.779 ± 0.078	0.761 ± 0.101	0.849 ± 0.093	**0.843 ± 0.144**	0.841 ± 0.091	0.831 ± 0.152
Right Common Iliac Artery	**0.811 ± 0.078**	**0.834 ± 0.139**	0.797 ± 0.071	0.805 ± 0.128	0.738 ± 0.059	0.751 ± 0.093	0.805 ± 0.081	0.831 ± 0.141	0.795 ± 0.079	0.806 ± 0.132
Left Common Iliac Artery	0.807 ± 0.075	0.827 ± 0.132	0.798 ± 0.071	0.813 ± 0.125	0.742 ± 0.056	0.759 ± 0.093	**0.808 ± 0.076**	**0.829 ± 0.136**	0.793 ± 0.072	0.807 ± 0.129
Right Internal Iliac Artery	**0.614 ± 0.198**	**0.721 ± 0.218**	0.597 ± 0.201	0.707 ± 0.223	0.521 ± 0.153	0.635 ± 0.171	0.607 ± 0.196	0.715 ± 0.217	0.599 ± 0.202	0.711 ± 0.221
Left Internal Iliac Artery	**0.612 ± 0.205**	**0.708 ± 0.232**	0.599 ± 0.201	0.691 ± 0.215	0.538 ± 0.146	0.624 ± 0.173	0.601 ± 0.202	0.703 ± 0.228	0.603 ± 0.196	0.705 ± 0.219
Right External Iliac Artery	**0.762 ± 0.099**	**0.838 ± 0.115**	0.751 ± 0.107	0.827 ± 0.126	0.689 ± 0.076	0.759 ± 0.093	0.758 ± 0.102	0.837 ± 0.117	0.754 ± 0.104	0.831 ± 0.124
Left External Iliac Artery	**0.755 ± 0.088**	**0.831 ± 0.115**	0.753 ± 0.085	0.827 ± 0.109	0.658 ± 0.069	0.738 ± 0.084	0.749 ± 0.079	0.829 ± 0.111	0.745 ± 0.075	0.821 ± 0.109
Overall	**0.684 ± 0.127**	**0.709 ± 0.153**	0.668 ± 0.101	0.693 ± 0.113	0.614 ± 0.095	0.639 ± 0.103	0.681 ± 0.098	0.707 ± 0.114	0.666 ± 0.100	0.694 ± 0.112

The ablation studies (Table 5 conducted in this work demonstrate the effectiveness of the proposed two-step segmentation strategy and highlight the contributions of various training components. Across most anatomical regions, the two-step approach consistently outperformed the single-step baseline. This improvement is particularly notable in smaller and more complex structures, where the second-stage refinement enables more precise boundary delineation and reduces segmentation errors. The hierarchical nature of the pipeline allows the model to first localize the region of interest and then focus on fine-grained details, which is especially beneficial in anatomically challenging areas.

Further experiments (Table 5 revealed that applying data augmentation in both stages of the two-step pipeline improves generalization, particularly in regions with high anatomical variability. Increasing the patch size from

$128 \times 128 \times 128$ to $192 \times 192 \times 192$ in the second step provided additional contextual information, which translated into higher DSC and NSD scores. Moreover, incorporating class-aware sampling during training helped mitigate the imbalance between large and small structures, leading to more consistent performance across all classes.

The proposed method performs well in regions with clear anatomical boundaries and sufficient spatial context, such as the descending aorta and iliac arteries. In these cases, the model benefits from both the global localization in the first step and the detailed refinement in the second step. However, segmentation errors are more frequent in small, closely adjacent structures, such as the renal arteries and proximal aortic zones. These failures are likely due to the difficulty in distinguishing subtle boundaries, limited resolution in the input data, and the inherent challenge of balancing the learning signal across structures of varying sizes. The current architecture and loss formulation may still favor larger regions, despite the use of class sampling.

These findings suggest that while the two-step strategy significantly improves segmentation performance, further enhancements—such as adaptive loss functions or attention-based mechanisms—may be necessary to fully address the challenges posed by small and ambiguous anatomical structures.

Table 5. Ablation study comparing single-step (SS) and two-step (DS) segmentation using ResUNet on the internal validation set. The analysis includes the effects of data augmentation, patch size, and class sampling. Results are reported as mean DSC and NSD scores (mean ± standard deviation) over 5-fold cross-validation.

Anatomical Region	SS 192^3		DS 192^3		DS 192^3 (Augmented)		DS 128^3 (Augmented)		DS 192^3 (Augmented + Sampled)	
	DSC ↑	NSD ↑	DSC ↑	NSD ↑	DSC ↑	NSD ↑	DSC ↑	NSD ↑	DSC ↑	NSD ↑
Zone 0	0.842 ± 0.072	0.758 ± 0.115	0.871 ± 0.061	0.774 ± 0.108	**0.895 ± 0.049**	0.819 ± 0.095	0.819 ± 0.072	0.742 ± 0.123	0.892 ± 0.052	**0.825 ± 0.092**
Innominate	0.671 ± 0.168	0.725 ± 0.182	0.715 ± 0.139	0.743 ± 0.158	0.732 ± 0.147	0.787 ± 0.157	0.684 ± 0.172	0.725 ± 0.161	**0.774 ± 0.119**	**0.836 ± 0.165**
Zone 1	0.539 ± 0.154	0.495 ± 0.161	0.554 ± 0.148	0.503 ± 0.151	0.591 ± 0.139	0.552 ± 0.143	0.502 ± 0.172	0.483 ± 0.173	**0.615 ± 0.141**	0.573 ± 0.152
Left Common Carotid	0.707 ± 0.128	0.819 ± 0.124	0.734 ± 0.123	0.828 ± 0.117	0.739 ± 0.121	0.829 ± 0.114	0.692 ± 0.112	0.745 ± 0.133	**0.752 ± 0.103**	**0.874 ± 0.102**
Zone 2	0.623 ± 0.133	0.521 ± 0.164	0.645 ± 0.128	0.545 ± 0.138	0.651 ± 0.125	0.548 ± 0.132	0.608 ± 0.141	0.504 ± 0.151	**0.667 ± 0.127**	0.558 ± 0.142
Left Subclavian Artery	0.731 ± 0.072	0.831 ± 0.098	0.775 ± 0.079	0.852 ± 0.102	0.781 ± 0.077	0.859 ± 0.103	0.717 ± 0.069	0.824 ± 0.089	**0.807 ± 0.074**	**0.885 ± 0.092**
Zone 3	0.615 ± 0.158	0.496 ± 0.152	0.627 ± 0.169	0.512 ± 0.181	0.634 ± 0.165	0.513 ± 0.172	0.612 ± 0.152	0.495 ± 0.148	**0.662 ± 0.156**	0.527 ± 0.157
Zone 4	0.729 ± 0.115	0.607 ± 0.131	0.751 ± 0.119	0.625 ± 0.137	**0.755 ± 0.113**	**0.627 ± 0.133**	0.739 ± 0.127	0.615 ± 0.141	0.749 ± 0.115	0.621 ± 0.134
Zone 5	0.854 ± 0.041	0.815 ± 0.088	0.891 ± 0.049	0.848 ± 0.101	**0.894 ± 0.046**	**0.853 ± 0.104**	0.851 ± 0.039	0.813 ± 0.082	0.887 ± 0.042	0.842 ± 0.091
Zone 6	0.639 ± 0.145	0.581 ± 0.181	0.679 ± 0.135	0.627 ± 0.172	0.691 ± 0.131	0.639 ± 0.162	0.604 ± 0.148	0.557 ± 0.185	**0.729 ± 0.127**	**0.677 ± 0.171**
Celiac Artery	0.523 ± 0.148	0.646 ± 0.161	0.562 ± 0.139	0.726 ± 0.142	0.572 ± 0.141	0.741 ± 0.145	0.517 ± 0.158	0.631 ± 0.172	**0.607 ± 0.143**	**0.774 ± 0.148**
Zone 7	0.614 ± 0.145	0.572 ± 0.171	0.662 ± 0.137	0.615 ± 0.162	0.671 ± 0.131	0.629 ± 0.151	0.541 ± 0.142	0.501 ± 0.179	**0.697 ± 0.133**	**0.649 ± 0.153**
SMA	0.592 ± 0.171	0.715 ± 0.178	0.619 ± 0.154	0.749 ± 0.173	0.624 ± 0.159	0.754 ± 0.175	0.578 ± 0.167	0.692 ± 0.181	**0.651 ± 0.152**	**0.772 ± 0.151**
Zone 8	0.642 ± 0.128	0.635 ± 0.165	0.675 ± 0.114	0.667 ± 0.144	0.682 ± 0.117	0.674 ± 0.147	0.619 ± 0.132	0.615 ± 0.172	**0.712 ± 0.115**	**0.701 ± 0.145**
Right Renal Artery	0.623 ± 0.152	0.785 ± 0.168	0.663 ± 0.142	0.836 ± 0.153	0.668 ± 0.138	0.839 ± 0.147	0.615 ± 0.157	0.782 ± 0.172	**0.682 ± 0.141**	**0.851 ± 0.153**
Left Renal Artery	0.576 ± 0.167	0.702 ± 0.198	0.611 ± 0.150	0.742 ± 0.164	0.615 ± 0.151	0.754 ± 0.165	0.557 ± 0.171	0.674 ± 0.204	**0.636 ± 0.142**	**0.787 ± 0.172**
Zone 9	0.852 ± 0.091	0.842 ± 0.139	0.894 ± 0.074	0.891 ± 0.123	**0.907 ± 0.069**	**0.898 ± 0.119**	0.824 ± 0.082	0.787 ± 0.131	0.899 ± 0.071	0.893 ± 0.121
Right Common Iliac Artery	0.811 ± 0.078	0.834 ± 0.139	0.828 ± 0.064	0.862 ± 0.102	0.829 ± 0.062	0.861 ± 0.098	0.789 ± 0.113	0.821 ± 0.159	**0.842 ± 0.078**	**0.878 ± 0.114**
Left Common Iliac Artery	0.807 ± 0.075	0.827 ± 0.132	0.832 ± 0.078	0.868 ± 0.114	0.833 ± 0.082	0.865 ± 0.119	0.778 ± 0.125	0.804 ± 0.167	**0.851 ± 0.084**	**0.888 ± 0.114**
Right Internal Iliac Artery	0.614 ± 0.198	0.721 ± 0.218	0.669 ± 0.201	0.812 ± 0.184	0.674 ± 0.205	0.815 ± 0.191	0.628 ± 0.208	0.748 ± 0.221	**0.721 ± 0.192**	**0.858 ± 0.202**
Left Internal Iliac Artery	0.612 ± 0.205	0.708 ± 0.232	0.675 ± 0.194	0.815 ± 0.175	0.682 ± 0.192	0.821 ± 0.173	0.635 ± 0.217	0.741 ± 0.253	**0.701 ± 0.186**	**0.841 ± 0.154**
Right External Iliac Artery	0.762 ± 0.099	0.838 ± 0.115	0.794 ± 0.075	0.852 ± 0.094	0.802 ± 0.078	0.864 ± 0.092	0.751 ± 0.102	0.831 ± 0.117	**0.831 ± 0.084**	**0.915 ± 0.098**
Left External Iliac Artery	0.755 ± 0.088	0.831 ± 0.115	0.801 ± 0.065	0.862 ± 0.077	0.804 ± 0.068	0.879 ± 0.078	0.741 ± 0.092	0.824 ± 0.122	**0.839 ± 0.071**	**0.929 ± 0.081**
Overall	0.684 ± 0.127	0.709 ± 0.153	0.719 ± 0.119	0.746 ± 0.138	0.727 ± 0.118	0.757 ± 0.135	0.670 ± 0.133	0.694 ± 0.158	**0.748 ± 0.115**	**0.781 ± 0.126**

4.1   Qualitative Results on Internal Validation Set

Exemplary segmentation results are presented in Fig. 2, showcasing both correctly and incorrectly segmented samples along with their respective performance scores.

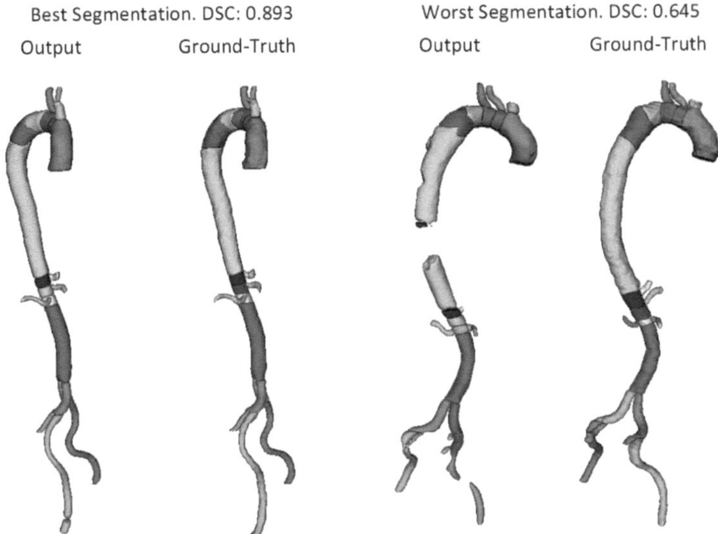

Fig. 2. Exemplary results from the internal validation set showing the best and the worst segmented cases (compared using the multiclass DSC). Note that the internal validation was performed without fold aggregation, resulting in worse performance than on the closed test set.

Most segmentation errors occur in small anatomical structures or when the first segmentation step fails due to out-of-distribution anatomical anomalies. These failures are primarily due to the difficulty in distinguishing fine-grained boundaries between adjacent aortic components. Additionally, the proposed architecture and training objective tend to prioritize larger structures, making it challenging to assign equal importance to smaller regions. This imbalance affects the model's ability to accurately capture fine details, especially in complex or ambiguous areas.

4.2   Results on Final Testing Set

The final results of the best-performing model on the final testing set are presented in Table 6, alongside a comparison with the baseline method introduced by the challenge organizers [7]. The table reports the average DSC and NSD in 40 test images for each anatomical region. All evaluations were conducted on the Grand-Challenge platform to ensure unbiased and standardized assessment.

The proposed method outperforms the baseline in all anatomical regions except Zone 6, Zone 7, the Superior Mesenteric Artery (SMA) and the Right Renal Artery (RRA). However, the performance differences for SMA and RRA are marginal. In particular, SMA and Zones 6 and 7 are relatively small structures with ambiguous boundaries, which may contribute to the observed discrepancies. For all other regions, particularly the upper aorta, the proposed method demonstrates superior performance over the baseline.

Table 6. Quantitative evaluation on the AortaSeg24 testing dataset. The table reports average DSC and NSD scores (mean ± standard deviation) across all 40 test cases for each anatomical region. The results were calculated directly using the Grand-Challenge platform to ensure unbiased assessment.

Anatomical Region	Our Method		Baseline Method [7]	
	Avg. DSC ↑	Avg. NSD ↑	Avg. DSC ↑	Avg. NSD ↑
Zone 0	**0.904 ± 0.049**	**0.827 ± 0.097**	0.880 ± 0.064	0.773 ± 0.119
Innominate	**0.766 ± 0.146**	**0.824 ± 0.157**	0.691 ± 0.164	0.739 ± 0.175
Zone 1	**0.629 ± 0.155**	**0.580 ± 0.140**	0.604 ± 0.164	0.560 ± 0.150
Left Common Carotid	**0.772 ± 0.104**	**0.891 ± 0.099**	0.743 ± 0.108	0.837 ± 0.117
Zone 2	**0.681 ± 0.124**	**0.554 ± 0.134**	0.659 ± 0.143	0.543 ± 0.153
Left Subclavian Artery	**0.803 ± 0.069**	**0.876 ± 0.086**	0.789 ± 0.115	0.859 ± 0.115
Zone 3	**0.675 ± 0.148**	**0.544 ± 0.145**	0.660 ± 0.171	0.517 ± 0.181
Zone 4	**0.768 ± 0.108**	**0.635 ± 0.129**	0.746 ± 0.122	0.620 ± 0.139
Zone 5	**0.903 ± 0.037**	**0.855 ± 0.083**	0.879 ± 0.054	0.826 ± 0.096
Zone 6	0.705 ± 0.129	0.650 ± 0.164	**0.731 ± 0.123**	**0.678 ± 0.164**
Celiac Artery	**0.614 ± 0.142**	**0.795 ± 0.141**	0.568 ± 0.178	0.728 ± 0.168
Zone 7	0.695 ± 0.128	0.656 ± 0.149	**0.699 ± 0.116**	**0.660 ± 0.146**
SMA	0.667 ± 0.146	**0.794 ± 0.144**	**0.678 ± 0.131**	0.782 ± 0.135
Zone 8	**0.707 ± 0.112**	**0.700 ± 0.140**	0.664 ± 0.160	0.656 ± 0.160
Right Renal Artery	0.695 ± 0.143	**0.867 ± 0.151**	**0.697 ± 0.142**	0.851 ± 0.140
Left Renal Artery	**0.625 ± 0.202**	**0.786 ± 0.202**	0.593 ± 0.199	0.742 ± 0.216
Zone 9	**0.901 ± 0.067**	**0.891 ± 0.118**	0.879 ± 0.081	0.860 ± 0.130
Right Common Iliac Artery	**0.857 ± 0.075**	**0.906 ± 0.095**	0.800 ± 0.132	0.840 ± 0.148
Left Common Iliac Artery	**0.853 ± 0.057**	**0.915 ± 0.087**	0.786 ± 0.135	0.842 ± 0.164
Right Internal Iliac Artery	**0.755 ± 0.111**	**0.881 ± 0.112**	0.661 ± 0.167	0.773 ± 0.179
Left Internal Iliac Artery	**0.686 ± 0.195**	**0.813 ± 0.207**	0.640 ± 0.197	0.767 ± 0.205
Right External Iliac Artery	**0.842 ± 0.106**	**0.933 ± 0.104**	0.789 ± 0.134	0.846 ± 0.143
Left External Iliac Artery	**0.852 ± 0.069**	**0.943 ± 0.068**	0.783 ± 0.151	0.851 ± 0.160
Overall	**0.755 ± 0.038**	**0.788 ± 0.042**	0.723 ± 0.058	0.746 ± 0.067

4.3   Limitation and Future Work

While our data-centric approach demonstrated strong performance across most anatomical zones, several limitations remain. First, the reliance on classical 3D RUNet architectures, although effective in low-data regimes, may limit scalability and adaptability to more complex or heterogeneous datasets. Additionally, our method showed reduced accuracy in smaller or more ambiguous structures, where architectural innovations or attention mechanisms might offer improvements.

Another key limitation lies in the annotation process. Manual labeling of aortic structures is time-consuming, requires expert knowledge, and is prone to variability between annotators. These inter-observer differences can introduce noise into the training data and complicate model evaluation, particularly in anatomically complex or poorly defined regions.

For future work, we plan to explore hybrid architectures that combine the robustness of classical models with the flexibility of transformer-based modules. We also aim to incorporate semi-supervised learning techniques to better leverage unlabeled data and improve performance in underrepresented regions. Furthermore, we intend to validate our approach on broader, multi-center datasets and investigate consensus-driven or probabilistic labeling strategies to mitigate annotation inconsistencies and improve generalizability.

5   Conclusion

In this work, we addressed the challenge of multiclass aortic segmentation by adopting a data-centric approach that emphasizes preprocessing, two-step segmentation, augmentation, and postprocessing over architectural complexity. Building on the classical 3D RUNet backbone, we demonstrated that careful engineering and training strategies can yield state-of-the-art performance, even in data-constrained settings.

Our results on the AortaSeg final test set (DSC 0.755 ± 0.038, NSD 0.788 ± 0.042) confirm that robust data handling—such as patch-based training, class-aware sampling, and resolution-aware inference—can have a greater impact than adopting more recent, complex architectures. These findings reinforce the importance of revisiting and refining established models from the perspective of data quality and task-specific optimization.

Acknowledgments. We thank all data contributors for making the medical images publicly available, and GrandChallenge for providing the challenge platform. This study was conducted as part of the MICCAI 2024 AortaSeg24 Challenge. All data used was publicly available and anonymized. We gratefully acknowledge Polish high-performance computing infrastructure PLGrid (HPC Center: ACK Cyfronet AGH) for providing computer facilities and support within computational grant no. PLG/2025/018194.

Disclosure of Interests. The authors have no competing interests to declare that are relevant to the content of this article.

Ethical Compliance Statement. All data used was publicly available and anonymized.

References

1. Pepe, A., Melito, G.M., Egger, J. (eds.): Segmentation of the Aorta. Towards the Automatic Segmentation, Modeling and Analysis of the Aortic Vessel Tree. LNCS (LNCS), MICCAI 2023 Workshop Proceedings. Springer (2023). https://doi.org/10.1007/978-3-031-53241-2
2. El-Ghotni, A., Nabil, M., El-Kady, H., Ayyad, A., Nasr, A.: A data-centric approach for segmenting the aortic vessel tree: a solution to SEG.A. Challenge 2023 segmentation task. In: Segmentation of the Aorta. Towards the Automatic Segmentation, Modeling, and Meshing of the Aortic Vessel Tree from Multicenter Acquisition. LNCS, vol. 14539, pp. 19–41. Springer (2024). https://doi.org/10.1007/978-3-031-53241-2_3
3. Fantazzini, P., et al.: Multi-view convolutional neural networks for aortic lumen segmentation in CT angiography. Med. Image Anal. **65**, 101771 (2020). https://doi.org/10.1016/j.media.2020.101771
4. Guo, Y., et al.: SegMamba: recursive mamba for medical image segmentation. arXiv preprint arXiv:2401.03020 (2024)
5. Hatamizadeh, A., Nath, V., Tang, Y., Yang, D., Roth, H., Xu, D.: Swin UNETR: swin transformers for semantic segmentation of brain tumors in MRI images. arXiv preprint arXiv:2201.01266 (2022)
6. Hatamizadeh, A., Tang, Y., Yang, D., Roth, H.R., Xu, D.: UNETR: transformers for 3D medical image segmentation. arXiv preprint arXiv:2103.10504 (2021)
7. Imran, M., et al.: CIS-UNet: multi-class segmentation of the aorta in computed tomography angiography via context-aware shifted window self-attention. Comput. Med. Imaging Graph. **118**, 102470 (2024)
8. Imran, M., et al.: Multi-class segmentation of aortic branches and zones in computed tomography angiography: the AortaSeg24 challenge. arXiv preprint arXiv:2502.05330 (2025)
9. Isensee, F., Jaeger, P.F., Kohl, S.A., Petersen, J., Maier-Hein, K.H.: nnU-Net: a self-configuring method for deep learning-based biomedical image segmentation. Nat. Methods **18**(2), 203–211 (2021). https://doi.org/10.1038/s41592-020-01008-z
10. Krebs, J.R., et al.: Volumetric analysis of acute uncomplicated type B aortic dissection using an automated deep learning aortic zone segmentation model. J. Vasc. Surg. **80**(4), 1025–1034 (2024)
11. Mercuri, M., Narracott, A.J., Hose, D.R., Göksu, C.: An automatic method for aortic segmentation based on level-set methods using multiple seed points. In: Tavares, J.M.R.S., Natal Jorge, R.M. (eds.) ECCOMAS 2017. LNCVB, vol. 27, pp. 875–882. Springer, Cham (2018). https://doi.org/10.1007/978-3-319-68195-5_95
12. Myronenko, A., Yang, D., He, Y., Xu, D.: Aorta Segmentation from 3D CT in MICCAI SEG.A. 2023 Challenge. In: Segmentation of the Aorta. Towards the Automatic Segmentation, Modeling, and Meshing of the Aortic Vessel Tree from Multicenter Acquisition, vol. 14539, pp. 13–18. Springer Nature Switzerland (2024). https://doi.org/10.1007/978-3-031-53241-2_2
13. Oktay, O., et al.: Attention U-Net: learning where to look for the pancreas. arXiv preprint arXiv:1804.03999 (2018)
14. Pérez-García, F., Sparks, R., Ourselin, S.: TorchIO: a Python library for efficient loading, preprocessing, augmentation and patch-based sampling of medical images in deep learning. Comput. Methods Programs Biomed., 106236 (2021). https://doi.org/10.1016/j.cmpb.2021.106236. https://www.sciencedirect.com/science/article/pii/S0169260721003102

15. Vagenas, N., et al.: Deep learning for 3D biomedical image segmentation: a comprehensive review. IEEE Trans. Med. Imaging (2024). https://doi.org/10.1109/TMI.2024.1234567
16. Wodzinski, M., Müller, H.: Automatic aorta segmentation with heavily augmented, high-resolution 3D ResUNet: contribution to the SEG.A challenge. In: Segmentation of the Aorta. Towards the Automatic Segmentation, Modeling, and Meshing of the Aortic Vessel Tree from Multicenter Acquisition, vol. 14539, pp. 42–54. Springer (2024). https://doi.org/10.1007/978-3-031-53241-2_4
17. Wodzinski, Marek: Source Code (2024). https://github.com/MWod/AortaSeg_2024

AortaST: A Student-Teacher Framework for Multi-class Aortic Segmentation

Abdul Qayyum[1]([✉])(iD), Moona Mazher[2](iD), and Steven A. Niederer[1](iD)

[1] National Heart and Lung Institute, Imperial College London, London, UK
`a.qayyum@imperial.ac.uk`
[2] Hawkes Institute, Department of Computer Science, University College London,
London, UK

Abstract. Accurate segmentation of the aorta and its branches is essential for the diagnosis and treatment planning of vascular diseases. In this work, we propose a two-stage deep learning framework specifically designed for multi-class segmentation of the aorta and its primary branches. The first stage employs a self-supervised 3D Student-Teacher Learning Framework to pretrain the encoder on unlabeled medical images, enabling the model to learn rich anatomical representations without manual annotations. In the second stage, we fine-tune an xLSTM-based UNet architecture using the labeled training set from the AortaSeg24 Challenge, which consists of 50 annotated 3D computed tomography angiography (CTA) scans. The model is validated on 10 cases and evaluated on a hidden test set of 40 cases. Our method achieves an overall Dice score of 0.737 ± 0.08 on the test set, better than both the baseline xLSTM and the widely adopted nnUNet. The integration of xLSTM modules effectively captures both long-range dependencies and local spatial details, improving segmentation accuracy in complex vascular anatomies. This framework demonstrates robustness in anatomically challenging regions and efficient utilization of limited labeled data through self-supervised learning. Our findings highlight the clinical potential of combining self-supervised pretraining with advanced recurrent architectures to deliver scalable, reliable segmentation tools that support more accurate and informed vascular interventions.

Keywords: Aortic segmentation · Self-supervised learning · xLSTM UNet · Medical image analysis · Multi-class segmentation · Computed tomography angiography (CTA) · MICCAI AortaSeg24 Challenge

1 Introduction

Accurately delineating the aorta and its branch vessels plays a central role in modern cardiovascular imaging. Detailed anatomical information is essential for diagnosing vascular conditions such as aneurysms, dissections, and occlusive disease, as well as for planning surgical and endovascular interventions. Because the aorta functions as the main arterial pathway supplying oxygenated blood to

© The Author(s), under exclusive license to Springer Nature Switzerland AG 2026
M. Imran et al. (Eds.): AortaSeg 2024, LNCS 16399, pp. 74–86, 2026.
https://doi.org/10.1007/978-3-032-14246-7_7

vital organs, even small errors in its anatomical modeling can have significant clinical consequences. The increasing reliance on minimally invasive approaches has further underscored the importance of precise three-dimensional reconstructions of the aortic tree. However, conventional segmentation techniques often reduce the problem to a binary task, which is insufficient for distinguishing individual branch vessels required in complex treatment planning. To accelerate research in this area, the MICCAI Aortic Anatomy Segmentation Challenge [3] was launched, providing a common benchmark dataset and evaluation framework for multi-class segmentation of the aorta and its branches in 3D computed tomography angiography (CTA) [4]. Several deep learning-based approaches have been proposed for segmentation of medical images in general [5,6,8,10–17] and particularly for aortic segmentation in recent years [2–4]. For example, CIS-Net [2] employs context-aware strategies to enhance the performance of 3D aortic segmentation. Despite their effectiveness, these models often focus on binary segmentation of the aorta and do not explicitly differentiate among its branches. Moreover, they may struggle with anatomical variations, high vessel tortuosity, and pathology-specific challenges limiting their use in clinical scenarios where branch-specific measurements are essential.

To overcome these limitations, we propose a two-stage deep learning framework specifically designed for multi-class segmentation of the aorta and its thirteen primary branches. In the first stage, we adopt a self-supervised 3D Student-Teacher Learning Framework to improve feature representation, especially in data-scarce settings. The second stage involves fine-tuning an xLSTM [1] based UNet architecture, optimized to segment complex aortic anatomy. Our approach demonstrates improved accuracy over baseline models and offers greater robustness in anatomically challenging cases, contributing toward more clinically reliable aortic segmentation tools.

2 Method

Our proposed model consists of two distinct stages. In the first stage, we implemented a Self-Supervised 3D Student-Teacher Learning Framework to enhance feature extraction. In the second stage, we fine-tuned an xLSTM-based UNet [1] model specifically for the segmentation of the aorta. A detailed description of each stage is provided below. Figure 1 shows the overall pipeline of our proposed model.

2.1 Self-supervised 3D Student Teacher Learning Framework

In a self-supervised learning framework [7], the goal is to leverage the teacher model to improve the performance of the student model. The teacher model typically provides the "ground truth" or reference features, which the student model aims to replicate or align with. We used the following steps to train student teachers in 3D models. We adopt a self-supervised student–teacher framework to pretrain our model before supervised fine-tuning. In this setup, the teacher model provides reference embeddings, and the student model is trained to replicate these embeddings through feature alignment. For the self-supervised pre-training stage, we used the same 50 images from the challenge dataset that were later employed for supervised training. During self-supervised learning (SSL), however, we treated them as unlabeled data by discarding ground-truth masks. This allows the model to leverage additional representational learning prior to using the labels for fine-tuning. Importantly, no external unlabeled dataset was used in this work. Training process follows the following steps.

1. **Feature Extraction:** Given a model with multiple layers, we are interested in features extracted from specific layers of both the teacher and student models. Let $\mathbf{F}_T^{(l)}$ denote the features extracted from layer l of the teacher model, and $\mathbf{F}_S^{(l)}$ denote the features extracted from layer l of the student model. These features are extracted and used within the student-teacher model.

2. **Contrastive Loss Calculation:** In the self-supervised learning (SSL) framework, a common approach is to use a contrastive loss to align the features from the teacher and student models. Given two sets of features, $\mathbf{F}_T$ (teacher) and $\mathbf{F}_S$ (student), the contrastive loss function is defined to maximize the agreement between corresponding features and minimize the agreement between non-corresponding features.

$$\boldsymbol{F}_T \in \mathbb{R}^{N \times D}$$
$$\boldsymbol{F}_S \in \mathbb{R}^{N \times D} \tag{1}$$

Where N is the batch_size and D is the feature dimension. Normalized the features for both models.

$$\hat{\boldsymbol{F}}_T = \frac{\boldsymbol{F}_T}{\|\boldsymbol{F}_T\|_2}$$
$$\hat{\boldsymbol{F}}_S = \frac{\boldsymbol{F}_S}{\|\boldsymbol{F}_S\|_2} \tag{2}$$

Equation 2 Compute the similarity matrix using the dot product of normalized features using the following equation.

$$\mathbf{S} = \frac{\hat{\mathbf{F}}_T \cdot \hat{\mathbf{F}}_S^{\top}}{\tau} \tag{3}$$

Where τ is the temperature parameter, a hyperparameter that controls the scaling of similarities.

3. **Loss Calculation:** Extract positive and negative similarities.
   - Positive similarity is the diagonal of the similarity matrix (the similarity between corresponding features).
   - Negative similarity includes all off-diagonal elements.

$$\mathcal{L}_{\text{contrastive}} = -\frac{1}{N} \sum_{i=1}^{N} \log \left(\frac{\exp(S_{ii})}{\exp(S_{ii}) + \sum_{j \neq i} \exp(S_{ij})} \right) \tag{4}$$

Here, S_{ii} is the positive similarity for the i-th example, and $\sum_{j \neq i} \exp(S_{ij})$ represents the sum of the negative similarities.

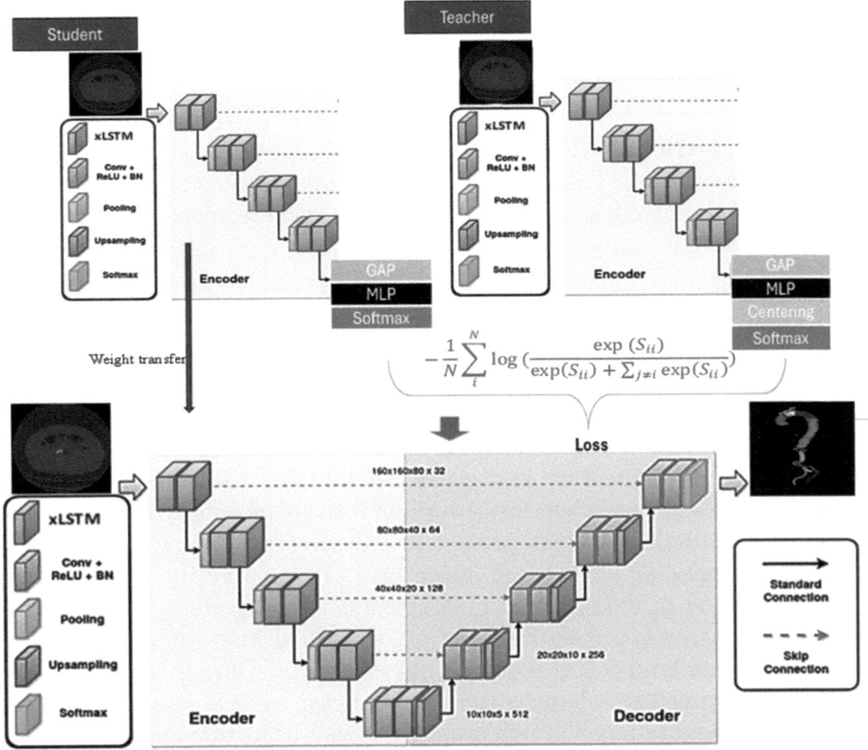

$$-\frac{1}{N}\sum_{i}^{N}\log\left(\frac{\exp\left(S_{ii}\right)}{\exp(S_{ii})+\sum_{j\neq i}\exp(S_{ii})}\right)$$

Fig. 1. Network architecture for proposed AortaST (A Student-Teacher Framework for Multi-Class Aortic Segmentation).

2.2 Proposed Network Architecture

The xLSTM-UNet model incorporates Vision-LSTM (xLSTM), an advanced evolution of Long Short-Term Memory (LSTM) networks. The xLSTM module has shown superior performance across multiple domains, including Natural Language Processing (NLP) and image classification, outperforming other approaches such as Vision Transformers and State Space Models (SSMs) like Mamba. Our architecture builds on xLSTM-UNet, which fuses UNet's encoder–decoder structure with Vision-LSTM (xLSTM) modules for long-range dependency modeling.

Pretrained Encoder: The encoder is pretrained in a self-supervised manner using the 50 challenge images (without labels). xLSTM enhances the encoder by capturing long-range dependencies and contextual information beyond local convolutions.

Fine-Tuned Decoder: After pretraining, the decoder is fine-tuned using the same 50 image–mask pairs, this time incorporating the ground-truth annotations to produce segmentation outputs.

Hybrid Local–Global Modeling: The combination of convolutional UNet layers and recurrent xLSTM units enables the model to simultaneously capture local details and global context—crucial for biomedical segmentation tasks such as aorta delineation.

Label Efficiency: By first pretraining with unlabeled forms of the challenge dataset, the model reduces dependence on large, labeled datasets while still achieving strong segmentation accuracy.

In this work, we propose a novel xLSTM with self-supervised learning (xLSTM-SSL) model for anatomical structure segmentation in medical imaging. The xLSTM architecture is designed to capture cross-slice dependencies through a lightweight recurrent framework, effectively modeling the spatial continuity and anatomical context present in volumetric scans capabilities often limited in conventional CNN-based approaches. To enhance the model's representation learning in data-scarce environments, we integrate a self-supervised pretraining strategy based on DINOv2 [9], a method known for its ability to extract rich, high-level features from unlabeled data. During the SSL phase, the model is exposed to a large corpus of unlabeled medical images and learns anatomical representations through proxy tasks such as feature matching, spatial alignment, and local-global consistency without relying on manual annotations. This pretraining equips the xLSTM-SSL model with strong anatomical priors, which translate into improved segmentation accuracy when fine-tuned on the limited labeled dataset.

3   Experiments

3.1   Dataset and Evaluation Protocol

We used the dataset and evaluation framework provided by the AortaSeg24 Challenge [3], organized as part of MICCAI 2024. The challenge focuses on multi-class segmentation of the aorta in computed tomography angiography (CTA), including 23 clinically relevant aortic branches and zones. The dataset consists of 100 annotated 3D CTA scans from patients with uncomplicated type B aortic dissection. Each volume was manually annotated by trained researchers and reviewed by an experienced vascular surgeon to ensure clinical accuracy. The annotations include major aortic branches (e.g., renal, iliac, and celiac arteries) and SVS/STS zones, following standard clinical guidelines. All volumes were resampled to an isotropic resolution of $1 \times 1 \times 1$ mm^3 for consistency of the 100 scans; 50 were provided for training. The remaining 50 were split between validation and hidden test sets by the organizers. The use of external datasets was not permitted during model development. To evaluate segmentation performance, we used two standard metrics:

1. Dice Similarity Coefficient (DSC) – quantifies volumetric overlap between predicted and reference segmentations.
2. Normalized Surface Distance (NSD) – measures the boundary accuracy within a 2 mm tolerance.

3.2   Implementation Details

1. **Data preprocessing:** During preprocessing, we normalize the input 3D CT angiography scans by clipping intensity values to a fixed range, followed by z-score normalization. All volumes are resampled to consistent voxel spacing, and non-zero regions are cropped to reduce computational overhead. To handle the high memory demand of large 3D inputs, we employ a patch-based inference strategy with overlapping windows, ensuring full-volume coverage while optimizing GPU usage. To train our model, we adopted a hybrid loss function combining Dice loss and Cross-Entropy (CE) loss. Dice loss mitigates the impact of class imbalance by directly optimizing overlap between predicted and ground-truth masks, while CE loss provides pixel-wise supervision that stabilizes training and enhances boundary delineation. Together, this combination ensures robust optimization across both large and small vascular structures. During inference, predictions from overlapping patches are aggregated using softmax averaging, followed by optional post-processing steps such as connected component filtering to refine the final segmentation output.
2. **Environment settings:** The development of environments and requirements is presented in Table 1. The training protocol used in our proposed model is shown in Table 2.

Table 1. Development of environments and requirements.

System: Ubuntu 20.04.6 LTS
CPU: AMD Ryzen Threadripper PRO 5955WX (16 cores / 32 threads)
RAM: 128 GB (16 × 8 GB), 2.67 MT/s
GPU: NVIDIA RTX A6000 48 GB
CUDA version: 12.2
Programming language: Python 3.8.3
Deep learning framework: PyTorch 2.0.1+cu118, Torchvision 0.15.2+cu118

Table 2. Training protocol using our proposed model.

Configuration	Details
Pre-trained Model	Trained based on SSL
Batch Size	12
Patch Size	$128 \times 128 \times 128$
Total Epochs	200
Optimizer	Adam
Initial Learning Rate (lr)	8×10^{-4}
LR Decay Schedule	MultiStepLR (gamma=0.1)
Gradient Accumulation Steps	20
Weight Decay	0.1
Loss Function	Dice+CELoss
Number of Model Parameters	24,867,472
Training Time	24 h
Image Size	128

4   Results and Discussion

In this work, we proposed an xLSTM-based U-Net architecture, evaluated both with and without self-supervised learning (SSL), and compared its performance against the state-of-the-art nnUNet model. The performance comparison was conducted on 10 validation cases from the official challenge leaderboard. As summarized in Table 3, the proposed xLSTM-SSL model consistently outperformed both the baseline xLSTM and the nnUNet across most anatomical regions, demonstrating the effectiveness of incorporating sequential modeling and SSL pretraining for improved segmentation accuracy in medical imaging. As evidenced in Table 3, xLSTM-SSL achieves superior performance across most vascular regions, outperforming both the xLSTM base model and the widely adopted nnUNet, with the highest overall Dice score of 0.7237. These results underscore the potential of combining xLSTM self-supervised learning to drive progress in robust and scalable medical image segmentation.

4.1   Qualitative Results on Validation Set

Figure 2 illustrates a good segmentation case, where the model's predicted segmentation closely matches the ground truth annotations. This strong overlap indicates that the model successfully identified the anatomical boundaries and structures of the aorta and its branches. However, minor discrepancies are still visible in certain anatomical classes. These small errors could be due to image noise, partial volume effects, or subtle anatomical variations between patients, which can make perfect segmentation challenging even for advanced models.

Despite these minor issues, the segmentation quality in this case is sufficient for most clinical or research purposes.

Table 3. Quantitative evaluation results for the validation cases (10) on the leader board dataset.

Anatomical Region	Avg. DSC (xLSTM-SSL)	Avg. DSC (xLSTM base)	Avg. DSC (nnUNet)
Zone 0	0.8462	0.8569	0.8241
Innominate	0.7696	0.7552	0.7650
Zone 1	0.6346	0.5986	0.5646
Left Common Carotid	0.5851	0.6650	0.6616
Zone 2	0.6975	0.6562	0.6406
Left Subclavian Artery	0.7268	0.7597	0.7387
Zone 3	0.7535	0.7294	0.7341
Zone 4	0.7657	0.7528	0.7526
Zone 5	0.8718	0.8609	0.8506
Zone 6	0.6976	0.6999	0.6877
Celiac Artery	0.6855	0.6681	0.6541
Zone 7	0.6444	0.6581	0.6460
SMA	0.6551	0.6399	0.6610
Zone 8	0.6577	0.6406	0.6271
Right Renal Artery	0.6835	0.6672	0.6519
Left Renal Artery	0.5626	0.5478	0.5043
Zone 9	0.8760	0.8663	0.8557
Right Common Iliac Artery	0.8245	0.7721	0.7626
Left Common Iliac Artery	0.8337	0.7976	0.8024
Right Internal Iliac Artery	0.7308	0.6531	0.7080
Left Internal Iliac Artery	0.7003	0.6433	0.6565
Right External Iliac Artery	0.7135	0.6865	0.6421
Left External Iliac Artery	0.7298	0.6622	0.6493
Overall	**0.7237**	**0.7060**	**0.6974**

In contrast, Fig. 3 illustrates a case of poor segmentation, where the model exhibits noticeable over-segmentation, particularly on the axial slice. Over-segmentation means the model predicted the structure beyond its true boundaries, possibly including adjacent tissues or artifacts as part of the segmented regions. This over-prediction causes distortions when reconstructing the 3D volume, leading to inflated or inaccurate representations of vessel sizes and shapes. Such errors can compromise downstream analyses, such as volume measurements or flow simulations, and may mislead clinical decision-making. Over-segmentation errors occur across multiple anatomical zones, suggesting that the model struggled to distinguish between closely adjacent or similar-appearing tissues in this case, possibly due to image quality, contrast variations, or complex vessel morphology.

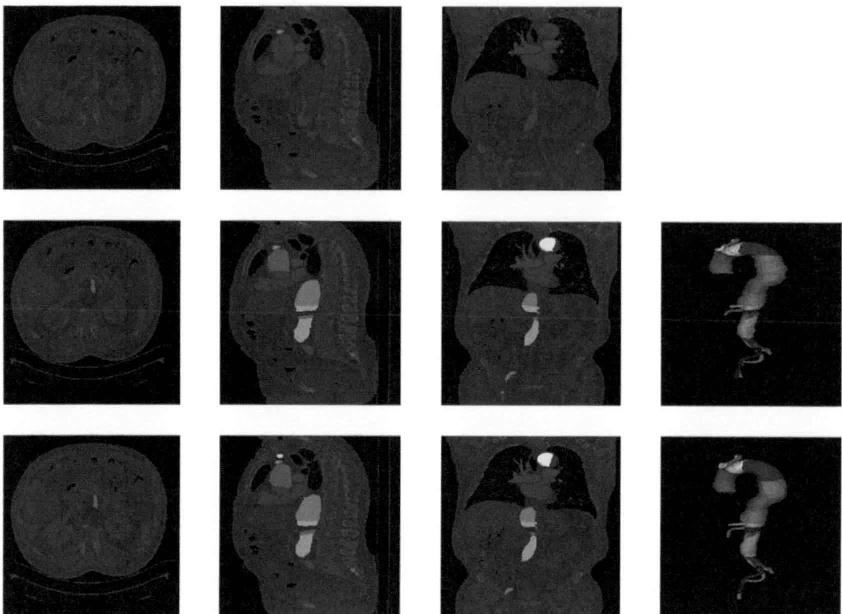

Fig. 2. Illustration of a successful segmentation case using our proposed model. The first row displays the raw input images, the second row shows the ground truth annotations, and the third row presents the segmentation results produced by our model.

4.2   Results on Final Testing Set

The performance of our proposed xLSTM-SSL model was evaluated on the final AortaSeg24 testing set and compared against the baseline method, CIS-UNet [2]. Table 4 presents the average Dice Similarity Coefficient (DSC) and Normalized Surface Distance (NSD) across 40 held-out test images for each anatomical structure. Our method consistently achieved higher scores than the CIS-UNet [3] in almost all anatomical regions. Substantial improvements were observed for the smaller and more challenging branch vessels (e.g., the left subclavian and right renal arteries), where the integration of self-supervised pretraining and long-range dependency modeling proved especially beneficial. These improvements indicate that the model effectively captures both global anatomical context and fine structural details, which are often missed by conventional CNN-based architectures. For larger vessels such as the ascending and descending aorta, performance gains were more modest, as both models already achieve relatively high accuracy in these regions. Nevertheless, the consistent increase in Dice and reduction in surface error across the full set of branches demonstrate the robustness of the xLSTM-SSL approach.

The Table 4 compares the performance of two models xLSTM-SSL (first column) and a CIS-UNet (second column) across various anatomical regions using the Dice Similarity Coefficient (DSC) metric. The xLSTM-SSL model, which

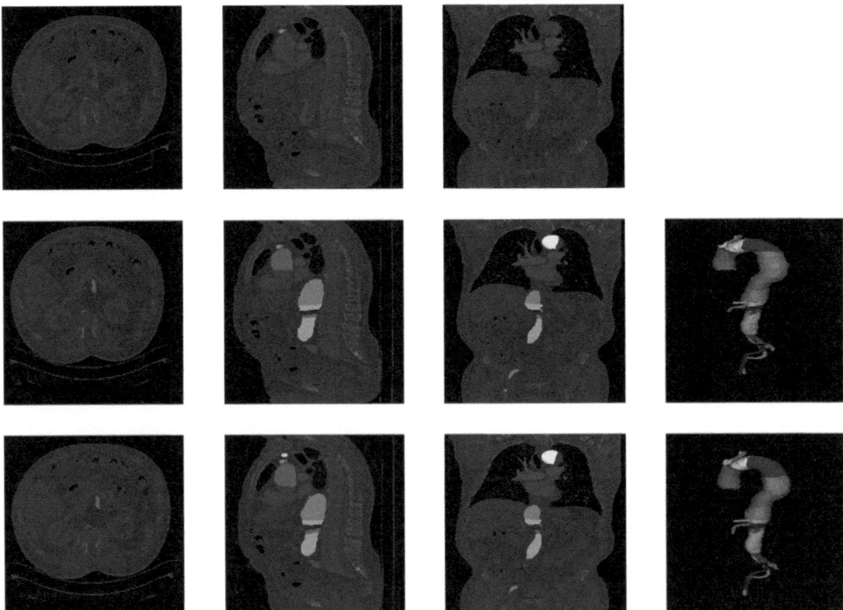

Fig. 3. Illustration of a challenging segmentation case using our proposed model. The first row shows the raw input images, the second row displays the ground truth annotations, and the third row presents the segmentation results produced by our model, which demonstrate visible errors in this case.

incorporates self-supervised learning, consistently outperforms the CIS-UNet in nearly all regions. This performance gain reflects the xLSTM-SSL model's improved ability to capture anatomical context and structure continuity. Overall, the table highlights the benefit of integrating sequential modeling and SSL in medical image segmentation tasks.

4.3   Limitation and Future Work

Although the proposed xLSTM-SSL model outperforms baseline approaches, there are some technical limitations worth addressing. The self-supervised pre-training was performed using only 50 unlabeled training images, which may limit the generalization capacity of the learned anatomical representations. Expanding the SSL phase to leverage a larger pool of unlabeled data could further improve model robustness. Additionally, the xLSTM architecture captures sequential information across slices but may not fully exploit long-range spatial dependencies; integrating attention-based modules or hybrid transformer-recurrent structures could enhance performance. Future work will also involve extending the approach to diverse anatomical structures and datasets, and exploring more advanced SSL tasks tailored for 3D medical imaging. Additionally, the current evaluation is restricted to a single dataset; future work will focus on validating generalizability across multi-center datasets and anatomical domains, and on optimizing the model for deployment in real-time clinical settings with constraints on computation and latency.

Table 4. Quantitative evaluation on the AortaSeg24 testing dataset. The table reports average Dice and NSD scores (mean ± standard deviation) across all 40 test cases for each anatomical region.

Anatomical Region	Our Method		CIS-UNet Method [2]	
	Avg. DSC	Avg. NSD	Avg. DSC	Avg. NSD
Zone 0	0.88±0.078	0.779±0.14	0.880 ± 0.064	0.773 ± 0.119
Innominate	0.754±0.141	0.802±0.161	0.691 ± 0.164	0.739 ± 0.175
Zone 1	0.616±0.186	0.557±0.181	0.604 ± 0.164	0.560 ± 0.150
Left Common Carotid	0.815±0.057	0.922±0.056	0.743 ± 0.108	0.837 ±0.117
Zone 2	0.677±0.133	0.566±0.157	0.659 ± 0.143	0.543 ± 0.153
Left Subclavian Artery	0.829±0.067	0.911±0.083	0.789 ± 0.115	0.859 ± 0.115
Zone 3	0.675±0.159	0.544±0.167	0.660 ± 0.171	0.517 ± 0.181
Zone 4	0.775±0.102	0.645±0.126	0.746 ± 0.122	0.620 ± 0.139
Zone 5	0.89±0.099	0.852±0.107	0.879 ± 0.054	0.826 ± 0.096
Zone 6	0.663±0.192	0.6±0.221	0.731 ± 0.123	0.678 ± 0.164
Celiac Artery	0.62±0.198	0.792±0.207	0.568 ± 0.178	0.728 ± 0.168
Zone 7	0.648±0.191	0.615±0.192	0.699 ± 0.116	0.660 ± 0.146
SMA	0.693±0.17	0.81±0.188	0.678 ± 0.131	0.782 ± 0.135
Zone 8	0.66±0.174	0.65±0.179	0.664 ± 0.160	0.656 ± 0.160
Right Renal Artery	0.705±0.167	0.857±0.193	0.697 ± 0.142	0.851 ± 0.140
Left Renal Artery	0.664±0.2	0.808±0.217	0.593 ± 0.199	0.742 ± 0.216
Zone 9	0.892±0.135	0.893±0.147	0.879 ± 0.081	0.860 ± 0.130
Right Common Iliac Artery	0.814±0.157	0.864±0.167	0.800 ± 0.132	0.840 ± 0.148
Left Common Iliac Artery	0.698±0.178	0.819±0.1	0.786 ± 0.135	0.842 ± 0.164
Right Internal Iliac Artery	0.767±0.104	0.894±0.1	0.661 ± 0.167	0.773 ± 0.179
Left Internal Iliac Artery	0.698±0.178	0.819±0.19	0.640 ± 0.197	0.767 ± 0.205
Right External Iliac Artery	0.725±0.158	0.798±0.164	0.789 ± 0.134	0.846 ± 0.143
Left External Iliac Artery	0.678±0.242	0.752±0.256	0.783 ± 0.151	0.851 ± 0.160
Overall	**0.737 ± 0.08**	**0.765 ± 0.087**	**0.723 ± 0.058**	**0.746 ± 0.067**

5   Conclusion

This work introduces a two-stage deep learning framework that significantly advances multi-class segmentation of the aorta and its key branches, addressing critical clinical challenges in vascular imaging. By harnessing self-supervised learning to pretrain on large unlabeled datasets, our model effectively captures complex anatomical features, even with limited annotated data. When fine-tuned on clinically validated CTA scans from the AortaSeg24 Challenge, the xLSTM-SSL model demonstrated superior accuracy and robustness compared to existing methods, including the widely used nnUNet. Improved segmentation precision across vital aortic branches and zones has the potential to enhance diagnostic confidence, surgical planning, and patient management in cases of aortic disease. Ultimately, this approach supports the development of reliable, scalable tools that can be integrated into clinical workflows, improving outcomes through more accurate and detailed vascular imaging analysis.

Acknowledgments. We thank all data contributors for making the medical images publicly available, and GrandChallenge for providing the challenge platform.

Disclosure of Interests. The authors have no competing interests to declare that are relevant to the content of this article.

Ethical Compliance Statement. All data used was publicly available and anonymized.

References

1. Beck, M., et al.: xLSTM: extended long short-term memory. Adv. Neural. Inf. Process. Syst. **37**, 107547–107603 (2024)
2. Imran, M., et al.: CIS-UNet: multi-class segmentation of the aorta in computed tomography angiography via context-aware shifted window self-attention. Comput. Med. Imaging Graph. **118**, 102470 (2024)
3. Imran, M., et al.: Multi-class segmentation of aortic branches and zones in computed tomography angiography: the aortaseg24 challenge. arXiv preprint arXiv:2502.05330 (2025)
4. Krebs, J.R., et al.: Volumetric analysis of acute uncomplicated type B aortic dissection using an automated deep learning aortic zone segmentation model. J. Vasc. Surg. **80**(4), 1025–1034 (2024)
5. Li, X., et al.: The state-of-the-art 3D anisotropic intracranial hemorrhage segmentation on non-contrast head CT: the instance challenge. arXiv preprint arXiv:2301.03281 (2023)
6. Luo, G., et al.: Tumor detection. Presented at the (2025)
7. Mazher, M., et al.: Self-supervised spatial-temporal transformer fusion based federated framework for 4D cardiovascular image segmentation. Inf. Fus. **106**, 102256 (2024)
8. Nan, Y., et al.: Hunting imaging biomarkers in pulmonary fibrosis: benchmarks of the AIIB23 challenge. Med. Image Anal. **97**, 103253 (2024)
9. Oquab, M., et al.: DINOv2: learning robust visual features without supervision. arXiv preprint arXiv:2304.07193 (2023)
10. Payette, K., et al.: Multi-center fetal brain tissue annotation (feta) challenge 2022 results. IEEE Trans. Med. Imaging (2024)
11. Qayyum, A., Ang, C.K., Sridevi, S., Khan, M.A., Hong, L.W., Mazher, M., Chung, T.D.: Hybrid 3D-ResNet deep learning model for automatic segmentation of thoracic organs at risk in CT images. In: 2020 International Conference on Industrial

Engineering, Applications and Manufacturing (ICIEAM), Sochi, Russia, 2020, pp. 1–5. IEEE (2020)

12. Qayyum, A., Razzak, I., Mazher, M., Lu, X., Niederer, S.A.: Unsupervised unpaired multiple fusion adaptation aided with self-attention generative adversarial network for scar tissues segmentation framework. Inf. Fus. **106**, 102226 (2024)

13. Qayyum, A., et al.: Transforming heart chamber imaging: self-supervised learning for whole heart reconstruction and segmentation. arXiv preprint arXiv:2406.06643 (2024)

14. de la Rosa, E., et al.: A robust ensemble algorithm for ischemic stroke lesion segmentation: generalizability and clinical utility beyond the isles challenge. arXiv preprint arXiv:2403.19425 (2024)

15. de la Rosa, E., et al.: ISLES'24: improving final infarct prediction in ischemic stroke using multimodal imaging and clinical data. arXiv preprint arXiv:2408.10966 (2024)

16. Yang, K., et al.: Benchmarking the CoW with the TopCoW challenge: topology-aware anatomical segmentation of the circle of Willis for CTA and MRA. ArXiv, arXiv–2312 (2025)

17. Zhang, M., et al.: Multi-site, multi-domain airway tree modeling. Med. Image Anal. **90**, 102957 (2023)

Accurate and Efficient Multi-class Segmentation for Aortic Branches and Zones in CTA

Kaixiang Yang[1,2], Yuxuan Luo[2], Qiang Li[1], and Zhiwei Wang[1(✉)]

[1] Wuhan National Laboratory for Optoelectronics, Huazhong University of Science and Technology, Wuhan, China
{kxyang,liqiang8,zwwang}@hust.edu.cn
[2] College of Life Science and Technology, Huazhong University of Science and Technology, Wuhan, China
yuxuanluo@hust.edu.cn

Abstract. The aorta is the largest artery of the body, pathology of the aorta and its main branches can be immediate threats to life or limb. Efficient and accurate segmentation of the aorta and its branches is conducive to assisting doctors to develop more appropriate diagnosis and treatment plans. Based on nnU-Net, we introduce a Channel-wised Sparse Self-Attention to enhance the network ability for tubular structure, and adopt an more efficient sliding window inference strategy to perform aorta segmentation. Experiments were conducted on AortaSeg24 challenge dataset. Our method achieves the mean DSC of 0.750 on 10 unseen validation images, and 0.752 on 40 unseen testing images. Codes are at https://github.com/Kaixiang-Yang/AortaSeg24.

Keywords: Multi-Class Segmentation · Aorta · Channel-wised Sparse Self-Attention

1 Introduction

The aorta is the largest artery in the human body, responsible for delivering oxygenated blood from the heart to the entire body, ensuring that various organs receive the necessary oxygen and nutrients [1]. Accurate segmentation of the aorta into standardized zones and branches is essential for assessing disease progression and planning interventions. Segmenting the aorta into standardized zones and branches allows for detailed regional analysis and enables clinicians to detect heterogeneous growth patterns along the aorta, supporting precise and personalized management of aortic diseases [2]. It also facilitates the analysis of related pathologies and improves the accuracy of imaging-based diagnoses, particularly in the early identification, diagnosis, and intervention of cardiovascular conditions.

K. Yang and Y. Luo—Co-first authors.

© The Author(s), under exclusive license to Springer Nature Switzerland AG 2026
M. Imran et al. (Eds.): AortaSeg 2024, LNCS 16399, pp. 87–96, 2026.
https://doi.org/10.1007/978-3-032-14246-7_8

However, translating this clinical potential into practice requires segmentation methods capable of meeting such fine-grained demands. Existing binary segmentation methods, which treat the entire aorta as a single homogeneous structure, have proven inadequate for a range of critical clinical applications. Tasks such as accurately determining the extent of aortic dissections, planning the placement of fenestrated endografts, and guiding the deployment of interventional devices require a much finer level of anatomical detail. In particular, these procedures demand precise, anatomically consistent delineation of both the segmented aortic zones and the branching vessels. To address this pressing need, the AortaSeg24 MICCAI Challenge [3] has been established as a standardized and open benchmark platform. It is designed to facilitate the development and rigorous evaluation of advanced multi-class aortic segmentation techniques, while simultaneously addressing the distinct challenges arising from the complex and highly variable morphology of vascular anatomy.

Building on the same motivation, many stable and reliable algorithms have emerged. Recent advances in deep learning have significantly improved 3D aortic segmentation in CT angiography. CIS-UNet [4] introduced a context-aware shifted window self-attention mechanism tailored for multi-class segmentation of the aorta, enabling precise delineation of anatomical zones and branches with improved long-range feature modeling. The nnU-Net framework [5] further provides a robust and self-configuring pipeline that automatically adapts to biomedical segmentation tasks without manual tuning, establishing a strong baseline for 3D aortic and vascular structure segmentation. Additionally, methods such as dynamic snake convolution [6] incorporate topological and geometric constraints to better capture the tubular morphology of vessels, enhancing the segmentation of complex and branching vascular structures.

Inspired by these developments and in response to the need for accurate aortic zone and branch segmentation to better support clinical decision-making and surgical planning, we propose an accurate and efficient multi-class segmentation method. Considering inference time and model parameters, we utilize the nnU-Net as our backbone and introduce a lightweight Channel-wise Sparse Self-Attention mechanism to enhance the segmentation performance of tubular structures. Additionally, a sliding window inference strategy is employed near the center of the image to reduce inference time consumption, taking into account the location of the aorta and its branches. Our method demonstrated solid performance on the AortaSeg24 validation set, achieving a mean Dice Similarity Coefficient of 0.750 on 10 unseen validation cases.

2   Method

2.1   Channel-Wised Sparse Self-Attention

In our previous work [7], we have designed a light-weighted and efficient channel-wised attention module named Channel-wised Sparse Self-Attention (CSSA) to enhance the interaction among feature channels. In this task, we adopt CSSA after the second convolution operation at each stage.

In detail, we define the features after the second convolution operation as $\mathbf{X} \in \mathbb{R}^{C \times D \times H \times W}$, and utilize a global average pooling (GAP) and two MLP layers to obtain scores $S \in \mathbb{R}^C$ for every channel, where the score S can be formulated as:

$$S = \mathbf{MLP}(\mathbf{GAP}(\mathbf{X})) \tag{1}$$

Then we sort S and have an indicator Q, where $Q(i) = j$, means that the j-th channel gets the i-th highest score, and $0 \le i, j < C$ ($i = 0$ means the highest). Next, we convert $Q(i)$ into a one-hot vector $\mathbf{e}_{Q(i)} = \mathbf{e}_j$, and construct a permutation matrix $\mathbf{P}$:

$$\mathbf{P} = \left(\mathbf{e}_{Q(0)}^{\mathrm{T}}; \, \mathbf{e}_{Q(1)}^{\mathrm{T}}; \, \ldots; \, \mathbf{e}_{Q(C_1-1)}^{\mathrm{T}} \right)^{\mathrm{T}} \in \mathbb{R}^{C \times C} \tag{2}$$

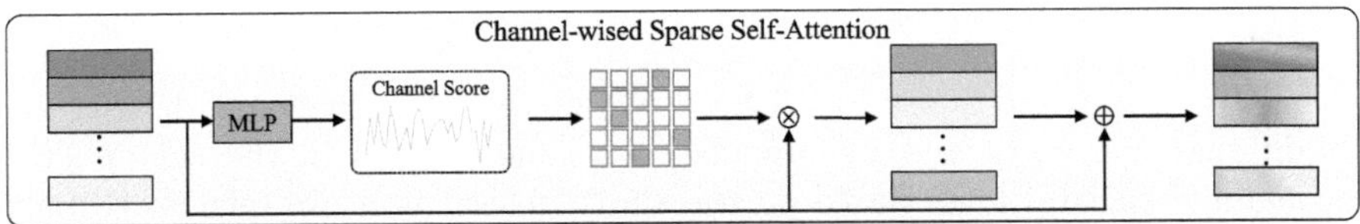

Fig. 1. The detail of CSSA.

Therefore, the final CSSA result can be written as, $CSSA(\mathbf{X}) = \mathbf{X} + \mathbf{P} * \mathbf{X}$, where $\mathbf{P}$ is sparse and can act as an attention matrix.

2.2 Network Backbone

We use nnU-Net [5] with deep supervision [8] as backbone, shown in Fig. 2. Moreover, 5, 4 and 4 down-sampling is operated in the vertival axis, coronal axis and sagittal axis, respectively. The four stages with the highest resolution are utilized for deep supervision during training phase. We combine the Dice loss and Cross Entropy loss to be our hybrid segmentation loss function which is the same as default of nnU-Net. Moreover, the compound loss function is usually robust in medical image segmentation [9].

2.3 Efficient Sliding Window Strategy

nnU-Net adopts sliding window inference strategy to obtain segmentation result of whole images because of the large image scale and memory limitation. The number of windows N depends on the image size (i_x, i_y, i_z), patch size (p_x, p_y, p_z), and step size s, and can be computed as follow:

$$N = \prod_{j}^{(x,y,z)} \left(\left\lceil \frac{i_j - p_j}{p_j \times s} \right\rceil + 1 \right) \tag{3}$$

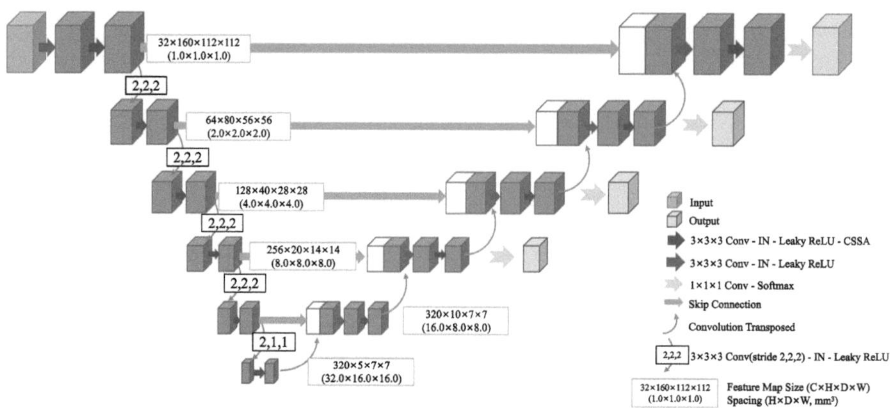

Fig. 2. Network architecture for aorta segmentation.

where $0 < s \leq 1$ and is set to 0.5 here. We observe the challenge dataset and obtain that the aorta and its branches are concentrated in the center along coronal and sagittal axis. Based on the above observation, we refer to [10] and revise the sliding window setting, as shown in Fig. 3,

$$Steps_q = \{i_q \times 0.5 + k \times p_q | k \in (-1.0, s-1, 0)\}, q \in \{x, y\} \tag{4}$$

only three start points along coronal and sagittal axis are considered which reduces more than 80% window number.

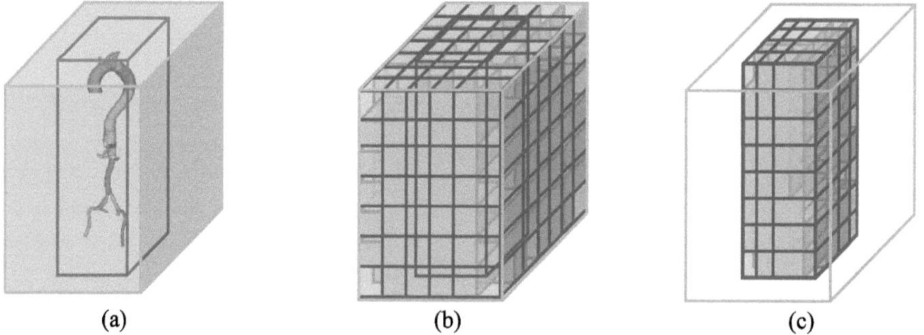

Fig. 3. Illustration of sliding window setting in inference. (a) Aorta and branches locate within red box. (b) Sliding window setting used in original nnU-Net. (c) Start points for each window (blue box) and window number along coronal and sagittal axis have been revised according to distribution of aorta. (Color figure online)

3 Experiments

3.1 Dataset and Evaluation Metrics

The Aorta Segmentation from CTA Volumes (AortaSeg24) provides 100 CTA images, consisting of 50, 10, 40 for training, validation and testing, respectively. For each patient, a CTA image is provided with 23 segmentation labels, containing aorta, its branches, and associated zones. The evaluation metrics encompass Dice Similarity Coefficient (DSC) and Normalized Surface Dice (NSD).

3.2 Implementation Details

Data Preprocessing. The data preprocessing pipeline includes normalization and random cropping in batches. All training cases are first resampled to the median voxel spacing of the dataset, using third-order spline interpolation for CT images and nearest-neighbor interpolation for the ground truth segmentations. The intensity of each CT volume is clipped between the 0.5 and 99.5 percentiles of the foreground voxels to reduce outlier effects, followed by Z-score normalization (subtracting the mean and dividing by the standard deviation). Finally, 3D patches of size $160 \times 112 \times 112$ are randomly cropped for training.

Environment Settings. The development environment are summarized in Table 1.

Table 1. Development environments and requirements.

System	Ubuntu 18.04.4 LTS
CPU	Intel(R) Core(TM) i7-10700 CPU @2.90GHz
RAM	251GB
GPU	Single NVIDIA GeForce RTX 4090 24G
CUDA version	12.0
Programming language	Python 3.8.17
Deep learning framework	torch 1.12.1, torchvision 0.13.1

Training Protocols. We adopt a series of data augmentation techniques to improve the robustness of the model, including rotations, scaling, Gaussian noise, Gaussian blur, brightness adjustment, contrast enhancement, and gamma correction. No additional data sampling strategy is applied beyond these augmentations. For model selection, we use the checkpoint of the final training epoch, which is then employed for both validation and submission to the final test stage. The detailed training configurations are summarized in Table 2.

Table 2. Training protocols.

Pre-trained Model	None
Batch size	2
Patch size	160×112×112
Total epochs	1000
Optimizer	SGD
Initial learning rate (lr)	0.01
Lr decay schedule	3e-5
Training time	23 h
Loss function	Dice + Cross Entropy
Number of model parameters	30.84M
Number of flops	462.06G

4   Results

4.1   Results on Validation Set and Final Testing Set

In the development stage, we use 50 training cases to train the model, and submit the last epoch checkpoint. The DSC of 23 structures are shown in Table 3. Ours performs 74.99% in average DSC, outperforming the official baseline more than 4% and ranking the 4th on the leaderboard. However, we observe that the DSC of **Left Renal Artery** in 2 cases is nearly 0%, leading to a lower average DSC,

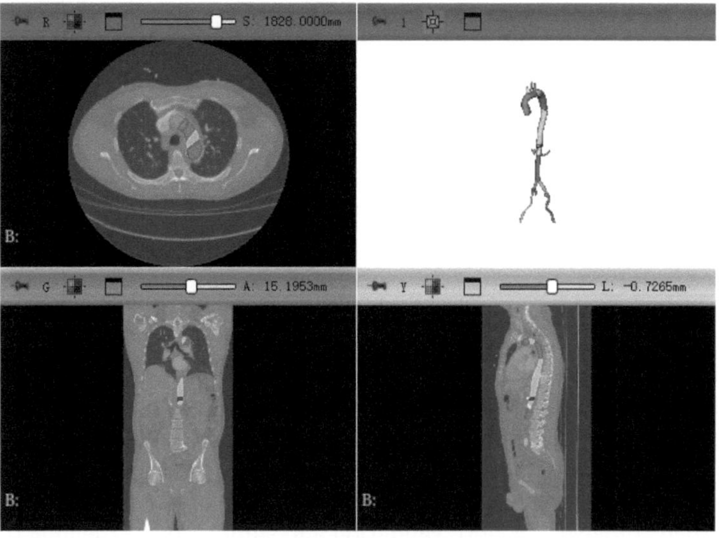

Fig. 4. Visualization of a training case.

Table 3. The average DSC of Aorta and branches on validation set.

Target	DSC	Target	DSC
Zone 0	0.877	SMA	0.620
Innominate	0.782	Zone 8	0.704
Zone 1	0.643	Right Renal Artery	0.665
Left Common Carotid	0.724	Left Renal Artery	0.557
Zone 2	0.729	Zone 9	0.880
Left Subclavian Artery	0.779	Right Common Iliac Artery	0.838
Zone 3	0.791	Left Common Iliac Artery	0.829
Zone 4	0.800	Right Internal Iliac Artery	0.731
Zone 5	0.886	Left Internal Iliac Artery	0.705
Zone 6	0.712	Right External Iliac Artery	0.806
Celiac Artery	0.694	Left External Iliac Artery	0.797
Zone 7	0.699	Avg Score	0.750

possibly due to poor image quality or anatomical variations in those patients. Since the validation cases are not available, we visualize one case of training data, as shown in Fig. 4.

On the final testing set of 40 CT angiography scans, our method outperformed the baseline CIS-UNet [4] in 18 of 24 anatomical regions for DSC and 21 for NSD, as shown in Table 4. In general, our approach achieved an average DSC of 0.752 ± 0.026 and NSD of 0.785 ± 0.033, improving on baseline scores of 0.723 ± 0.058 and 0.746 ± 0.067 respectively. These results demonstrate enhanced and consistent segmentation accuracy and surface alignment across diverse aortic zones and branch vessels, thereby indicating the robustness and reliability of our method when applied to challenging vascular structures.

4.2 Ablation Study

We conduct experiments on CSSA using the 10 validation set, where we systematically analyze the model parameters and floating point operations (FLOPs) for both variants of the network. The detailed quantitative results obtained from this comparison are presented in Table 5. From these results, it can be observed that the network with CSSA achieves consistently better performance, while at the same time not introducing an excessive number of parameters or FLOPs.

5   Discussion

The experimental results confirm the effectiveness of our proposed approach in improving segmentation performance without increasing model complexity. While the overall results are promising, some anatomically challenging regions such as zone 4, zone 5, zone 6, zone 7, and the Celiac Artery show relatively

Table 4. Comparison of Our Method with Baseline [4]

Anatomical Region	Our Method		Baseline Method [4]	
	Avg. DSC	Avg. NSD	Avg. DSC	Avg. NSD
Zone 0	**0.889** ± 0.059	**0.790** ± 0.131	0.880 ± 0.064	0.773 ± 0.119
Innominate	**0.718** ± 0.121	**0.765** ± 0.141	0.691 ± 0.164	0.739 ± 0.175
Zone 1	**0.644** ± 0.162	**0.593** ± 0.157	0.604 ± 0.164	0.560 ± 0.150
Left Common Carotid	**0.770** ± 0.089	**0.879** ± 0.089	0.743 ± 0.108	0.837 ± 0.117
Zone 2	**0.698** ± 0.133	**0.593** ± 0.158	0.659 ± 0.143	0.543 ± 0.153
Left Subclavian Artery	**0.810** ± 0.076	**0.883** ± 0.096	0.789 ± 0.115	0.859 ± 0.115
Zone 3	**0.683** ± 0.169	**0.564** ± 0.166	0.660 ± 0.171	0.517 ± 0.181
Zone 4	0.737 ± 0.133	**0.643** ± 0.136	**0.746** ± 0.122	0.620 ± 0.139
Zone 5	0.866 ± 0.068	**0.829** ± 0.089	**0.879** ± 0.054	0.826 ±0.096
Zone 6	0.694 ± 0.135	0.637 ± 0.177	**0.731** ± 0.123	**0.678** ± 0.164
Celiac Artery	0.562 ± 0.179	0.719 ± 0.171	**0.568** ± 0.178	**0.728** ± 0.168
Zone 7	0.677 ± 0.142	0.648 ± 0.163	**0.699** ± 0.116	**0.660** ± 0.146
SMA	**0.687** ± 0.116	**0.801** ± 0.119	0.678 ±0.131	0.782 ± 0.135
Zone 8	**0.677** ± 0.142	**0.668** ± 0.157	0.664 ± 0.160	0.656 ± 0.160
Right Renal Artery	**0.711** ± 0.134	**0.877** ± 0.146	0.697 ± 0.142	0.851 ± 0.140
Left Renal Artery	**0.677** ± 0.159	**0.839** ± 0.158	0.593 ± 0.199	0.742 ± 0.216
Zone 9	**0.915** ± 0.037	**0.914** ± 0.090	0.879 ± 0.081	0.860 ± 0.130
Right Common Iliac Artery	**0.860** ± 0.061	**0.912** ± 0.079	0.800 ± 0.132	0.840 ± 0.148
Left Common Iliac Artery	**0.866** ± 0.031	**0.932** ± 0.055	0.786 ± 0.135	0.842 ± 0.164
Right Internal Iliac Artery	**0.770** ± 0.086	**0.897** ± 0.091	0.661 ± 0.167	0.773 ± 0.179
Left Internal Iliac Artery	**0.695** ± 0.147	**0.822** ± 0.148	0.640 ± 0.197	0.767 ± 0.205
Right External Iliac Artery	**0.847** ± 0.064	**0.938** ± 0.058	0.789 ± 0.134	0.846 ± 0.143
Left External Iliac Artery	**0.832** ± 0.071	**0.913** ± 0.078	0.783 ± 0.151	0.851 ± 0.160
Overall	**0.752** ± 0.026	**0.785** ± 0.033	0.723 ± 0.058	0.746 ± 0.067

Table 5. Ablation study on validation set.

Methods	DSC ↑	Param(M) ↓	FLOPs(G) ↓
w/o CSSA	0.746	30.60	461.37
w/ CSSA	0.750	30.84	462.06

lower segmentation accuracy. These regions are typically small in size, exhibit high inter-subject variability, or are located at the periphery of the scan volume—factors that increase difficulty for both annotation and prediction. In addition, the current architecture may still have limited capacity in modeling fine-grained structural context in these peripheral or tubular regions, especially under a sliding window inference strategy.

In future work, we plan to explore the integration of large-scale foundation models such as the Segment Anything Model (SAM), along with tubular-structure-aware attention mechanisms, to further enhance segmentation accuracy in these anatomically difficult regions.

6 Conclusion

In this paper, we optimize the nnU-Net framework to enable accurate and efficient multi-class segmentation of the aorta and its branches in CTA scans. To enhance the model's ability to capture long-range dependencies and contextual anatomical structures, we integrate a CSSA module into the baseline architecture. With this modification, our method achieves a higher average DSC on the validation set, demonstrating improved segmentation accuracy across both major aortic zones and smaller branch vessels. Importantly, these gains are achieved without introducing a substantial increase in model parameters or computational complexity. Compared with the CIS-UNet baseline, our model offers better performance with lower inference-time cost.

Acknowledgements. We thank all data contributors for making the medical images publicly available, and GrandChallenge for providing the challenge platform. This work was supported by National Natural Science Foundation of China (Grant No. 62202189) and Wuhan United Imaging Healthcare Surgical Technology Co., Ltd. and conducted as part of the MICCAI 2024 AortaSeg24 Challenge.

Ethical Compliance Statement. All data used was publicly available and anonymized. As no new human or animal data were collected, institutional review board approval was not applicable.

Disclosure of Interests. The authors have no competing interests to declare that are relevant to the content of this article.

References

1. Members, W.C., et al.: 2022 ACC/AHA guideline for the diagnosis and management of aortic disease: a report of the American heart association/American college of cardiology joint committee on clinical practice guidelines. J. Am. College Cardiol. **80**(24), e223–e393 (2022)
2. Krebs, J.R., et al.: Volumetric analysis of acute uncomplicated type b aortic dissection using an automated deep learning aortic zone segmentation model. J. Vasc. Surg. **80**(4), 1025–1034 (2024)
3. Imran, M., et al.: Multi-class segmentation of aortic branches and zones in computed tomography angiography: the aortaseg24 challenge. arXiv preprint arXiv:2502.05330 (2025)
4. Imran, M., et al.: CIS-UNet: multi-class segmentation of the aorta in computed tomography angiography via context-aware shifted window self-attention. Comput. Med. Imaging Graph. **118**, 102470 (2024)

5. Isensee, F., Jaeger, P.F., Kohl, S.A., Petersen, J., Maier-Hein, K.H.: nnU-Net: a self-configuring method for deep learning-based biomedical image segmentation. Nat. Methods **18**(2), 203–211 (2021)
6. Qi, Y., He, Y., Qi, X., Zhang, Y., Yang, G.: Dynamic snake convolution based on topological geometric constraints for tubular structure segmentation. In: Proceedings of the IEEE/CVF International Conference on Computer Vision, pp. 6070–6079 (2023)
7. Yang, K., et al.: Decoupling feature representations of ego and other modalities for incomplete multi-modal brain tumor segmentation. In: 2024 IEEE International Conference on Bioinformatics and Biomedicine (BIBM), Lisbon, Portugal, 2024, pp. 3897–3902. IEEE (2024)
8. Lee, C.Y., Xie, S., Gallagher, P., Zhang, Z., Tu, Z.: Deeply-supervised nets. In: Artificial Intelligence and Statistics, pp. 562–570. PMLR (2015)
9. Ma, J., et al.: Loss odyssey in medical image segmentation. Med. Image Anal. **71**, 102035 (2021)
10. Huang, Z., et al.: Revisiting nnU-Net for iterative pseudo labeling and efficient sliding window inference. In: Ma, J., Wang, B. (eds) MICCAI Challenge on Fast and Low-Resource Semi-supervised Abdominal Organ Segmentation, pp. 178–189. Springer, Cham (2022). https://doi.org/10.1007/978-3-031-23911-3_16

Application of nnUnet for Multi-class Segmentation of Aortic Branches and Zones in CTA

Yuchong Gao, Hongye Zeng, Haoyu Zheng, and Rui Zheng(✉)

School of Information Science and Technology, ShanghaiTech University,
Shanghai, China
{gaoych,zhengrui}@shanghaitech.edu.cn

Abstract. The aorta plays a critical role in delivering oxygenated blood from the heart to the body. Accurate segmentation of aortic zones and branches in computed tomography angiography (CTA) is vital for diagnosis and surgical planning. We present our solution to the AortaSeg24 (https://aortaseg24.grand-challenge.org/) challenge (Multi-Class Segmentation of Aortic Branches and Zones in CTA), which targets the automatic segmentation of aortic anatomy from 3D CTA volumes. We adopted the nnUNetv2 (https://github.com/MIC-DKFZ/nnUNet/tree/master) framework for its strong generalization in medical image segmentation, training our model on the provided dataset with minimal manual tuning. On the hidden test set of 40 cases, our method achieved an average Dice score of **0.729 ± 0.043** and an average normalized surface Dice (NSD) of **0.751 ± 0.047**. High performance was observed in regions such as Zone 9 (Dice: 0.905 ± 0.048) and the Left Common Carotid Artery (Dice: 0.779 ± 0.094). All code used for training and evaluation has been made publicly available on GitHub (https://github.com/puppy1234/Aortaseg24_source_code). These results demonstrate the effectiveness of our nnUNetv2-based approach for large-scale aortic segmentation in clinical CTA data.

Keywords: Aortaseg24 · nnUnet · Segmentation · Aorta · Deep Learning

1 Introduction

The aorta, the largest artery in the human body, plays a vital role in delivering oxygenated blood from the heart to the head, neck, upper limbs, abdomen, pelvis, and lower extremities. Aortic diseases such as dissection, aneurysm, and atherosclerosis can lead to life-threatening complications and often require urgent diagnosis and surgical intervention [7]. With the advancement of medical imaging technologies, computed tomography angiography (CTA) has become a standard modality for non-invasive, high-resolution, 3D visualization of the aorta and its major branches [10]. CTA enables accurate assessment of vessel geometry,

M. Imran et al. (Eds.): AortaSeg 2024, LNCS 16399, pp. 97–108, 2026.
https://doi.org/10.1007/978-3-032-14246-7_9

including diameter and volume, which is critical for clinical decision-making and planning endovascular treatments such as stent graft implantation.

Segmenting the aortic zones and branches from CTA is essential for device selection, risk assessment, and surgical planning. However, manual segmentation is time-consuming and prone to inter-observer variability. Automated and accurate segmentation remains a challenging task due to the complex and variable aortic anatomy [6]. To address these limitations, the AortaSeg24 Challenge was launched as part of MICCAI 2024. It provides the first large-scale, publicly available dataset with 100 annotated CTA volumes, covering both aortic branches and SVS/STS zones. The challenge aims to advance multi-class segmentation techniques in CTA and ultimately improve clinical care, focus attention on underexplored diseases like auTBAD, and promote interdisciplinary collaboration in the medical image analysis community [4].

Automated segmentation of the aorta in CTA images plays a vital role in precise anatomical evaluation and device selection, particularly in the context of endovascular interventions. Early vascular segmentation approaches—such as edge detection, thresholding, and region growing—have been extensively studied, yet they often suffer from limited accuracy and robustness when applied to anatomically complex and variable structures like the aorta [9]. These traditional methods are highly sensitive to noise, image artifacts, and intensity inhomogeneity, and typically require extensive parameter tuning or manual correction, which limits their scalability and reliability in clinical workflows.

In recent years, deep learning has revolutionized medical image segmentation. Architectures such as U-Net [2], H-DenseUNet [8], and Swin-Unet [1] have demonstrated remarkable performance across a variety of medical image analysis tasks, including vascular segmentation. These models leverage hierarchical feature extraction and multi-scale learning to capture both global context and fine-grained anatomical details. Notably, CIS-Net [3] was specifically designed for 3D aortic segmentation, combining convolutional and transformer-based modules to enhance long-range dependency modeling and inter-class separation, achieving state-of-the-art performance in large-vessel segmentation tasks.

Despite these advances, many existing approaches still treat the aorta as a single anatomical unit, neglecting the clinically important subdivision into zones and branches. The lack of publicly available multi-class annotations for aortic structures has further limited the development and benchmarking of fine-grained segmentation algorithms. The AortaSeg24 Challenge aims to fill this gap by promoting research in multi-class, anatomically-aware segmentation of the aorta and its branches.

We employ the state-of-the-art nnU-Net v2 framework—known for its automated configuration and strong generalization—to build an end-to-end pipeline for multi-class segmentation of aortic anatomy in 3D CTA.

The key contributions of this work are as follows:

- Automated nnU-Net v2 adaptation. We show that nnU-Net v2, with minimal manual tuning, can be seamlessly tailored to segment both aortic zones and branch vessels on the AortaSeg24 dataset, yielding state-of-the-art accuracy.

- Comprehensive hidden-test evaluation. Our method achieves an average Dice score of 0.729 ± 0.043 and an NSD of 0.751 ± 0.047 over 40 unseen CTA volumes, with particularly high performance in Zone 9 (Dice $= 0.905 \pm 0.048$) and the Left Common Carotid Artery (Dice $= 0.779 \pm 0.094$).
- Open-source reproducibility. We release all training and inference scripts on GitHub, facilitating reproduction, adaptation to new datasets, and further clinical research.

These contributions establish a reliable, reproducible baseline for large-scale aortic segmentation in clinical CTA and lay the foundation for automated vascular analysis in both research and practice.

2   Method

Our method is implemented based on the open-source project nnU-Net, a deep learning framework designed for medical image segmentation tasks. One of the key features of nnU-Net is its ability to automatically configure the network architecture, preprocessing pipeline, training parameters, and post-processing strategies according to the given dataset [5]. This eliminates the need for manual network design and makes the framework highly adaptable and automated.

2.1   Network Architecture

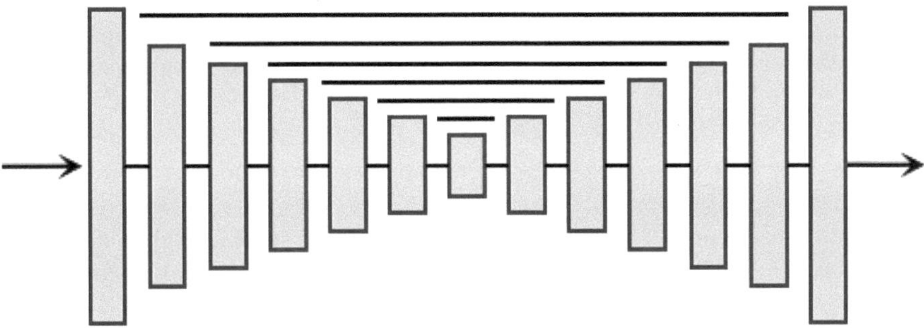

Fig. 1. Schematic of the U-Net backbone automatically configured by nnU-Net. It follows an encoderâĂŞdecoder design with skip connections for multi-scale feature fusion. The network consists of a contracting path (left side) and an expansive path (right side).

The network architecture used in this study is automatically configured by nnU-Net, which is essentially a tailored variant of the U-Net architecture(shown in Fig. 1). The specific structure is dynamically adapted based on the properties of the input dataset, such as image resolution, voxel spacing, and anatomical variability. In our case, nnU-Net selected the 3D full-resolution U-Net as the optimal configuration.

The architecture consists of a symmetric encoder–decoder structure, comprising the following key components:

- **Encoder:** Each encoder stage contains two consecutive 3D convolutional layers with kernel size $3 \times 3 \times 3$, followed by instance normalization and a leaky ReLU activation. A $2 \times 2 \times 2$ max pooling operation with stride 2 is applied at the end of each stage to perform downsampling and progressively reduce the spatial resolution while increasing the number of feature channels.
- **Decoder:** The decoder mirrors the encoder in structure. Each decoder stage begins with a transposed convolution for upsampling, followed by concatenation with the corresponding encoder feature map via skip connections. This is followed by two $3 \times 3 \times 3$ convolutional layers with the same normalization and activation functions as in the encoder.
- **Output layer:** A final $1 \times 1 \times 1$ convolutional layer is used to map the feature maps to the desired number of output segmentation classes.

In our case, nnU-Net selected the 3D full-resolution U-Net as the optimal configuration. The architecture follows a symmetric encoder–decoder design (Fig. 1), where downsampling progressively encodes contextual information and upsampling restores spatial resolution through skip connections. The final $1 \times 1 \times 1$ convolution produces voxel-wise class predictions.

Instead of manually tuning hyperparameters, nnU-Net automatically determines critical settings such as patch size, input spacing, and network depth based on dataset-specific properties (e.g., voxel resolution and anatomical variability). This automated design reduces heuristic bias and ensures strong generalization.

2.2   Loss Function and Inference Strategy

Loss Function. We adopted the default compound loss function used in nnU-Net, which is a weighted combination of Dice loss and Cross-Entropy (CE) loss. This composite formulation is particularly effective in handling class imbalance between foreground and background regions, a common challenge in medical image segmentation tasks. The total loss is defined as:

$$\mathcal{L} = \lambda_1 \cdot \mathcal{L}_{\text{Dice}} + \lambda_2 \cdot \mathcal{L}_{\text{CE}} \tag{1}$$

where $\lambda_1 = \lambda_2 = 1$ in our implementation.

Inference Strategy. Due to the high memory consumption of volumetric medical data, nnU-Net automatically applies a sliding window inference strategy and a patch-wise training approach. These techniques enable processing of large images by dividing them into manageable sub-volumes, thereby avoiding GPU memory overflow. Additionally, test-time augmentation (TTA) based on mirroring is employed to enhance prediction robustness and reduce variance in the inference stage.

3   Experiments

3.1   Dataset and Evaluation Protocol

We used the dataset and evaluation framework provided by the AortaSeg24 Challenge [4], organized as part of MICCAI 2024. The challenge focuses on multi-class segmentation of the aorta in computed tomography angiography (CTA), including 23 clinically relevant aortic branches and zones. The dataset consists of 100 annotated 3D CTA scans from patients with uncomplicated type B aortic dissection. Each volume was manually annotated by trained researchers and reviewed by an experienced vascular surgeon to ensure clinical accuracy. The annotations include major aortic branches (e.g., renal, iliac, and celiac arteries) and SVS/STS zones, following standard clinical guidelines. All volumes were resampled to an isotropic resolution of $1 \times 1 \times 1$ mm^3 for consistency. We show an example of the data in Fig. 2.

Of the 100 scans, 50 were provided for training. The remaining 50 were split between validation and hidden test sets by the organizers. The use of external datasets was not permitted during model development. All data used was publicly available and anonymized, and this study was approved by our local IRB with ethics number: Shanghaitech SISR IRB#2021-003.

To evaluate segmentation performance, we used two standard metrics:

1. **Dice Similarity Coefficient (DSC)** âĂŞ quantifies volumetric overlap between predicted and reference segmentations.
2. **Normalized Surface Distance (NSD)** âĂŞ measures the boundary accuracy within a 2 mm tolerance.

3.2   Implementation Details

Data Preprocessing. The preprocessing pipeline in nnU-Net is fully automated and requires no manual intervention. Once the dataset is organized following the required folder structure, preprocessing is executed by running the following command:

```
python nnUNetv2_plan_and_preprocess -d DATASET_ID
```

Here, `DATASET_ID` refers to the identifier corresponding to the dataset directory. Upon execution, nnU-Net performs a series of standardized preprocessing steps, including:

- **Cropping:** Automatic foreground detection is used to crop unnecessary background regions.
- **Resampling:** All images are resampled to a uniform voxel spacing determined from the dataset statistics.
- **Normalization:** Intensity normalization is applied independently to each image, using either z-score or percentile-based strategies depending on the modality.

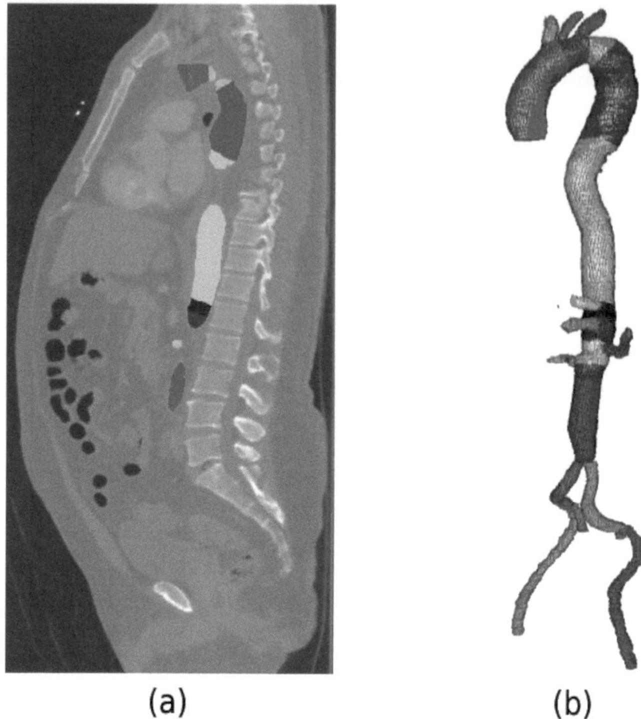

Fig. 2. Aortaseg24 data example. (a) Sagittal slice of the CTA data. (b) 3D rendering of 23 different aorta zones.

The preprocessed data is saved in a dedicated subfolder within the **nnUNet _preprocessed** directory, named after the dataset ID. Two configuration files, namely **dataset_fingerprint.json** and **nnUNetPlans.json**, are also automatically generated along with the preprocessed data. These store metadata and network configuration parameters inferred from the dataset. During inference, the same preprocessing pipeline is applied to ensure consistency between training and testing phases.

Environment Settings. The development environment and software requirements are summarized in Table 1.

Training Protocols. During the training of the nnU-Net, we employ extensive data augmentation, including 3D random rotations, scaling, elastic deformations, mirroring, as well as intensity perturbations like Gaussian noise, blurring, and contrast adjustments to improve generalization. A patch-based sampling strategy is used, which samples patches containing foreground regions to address class imbalance. The optimal model is selected based on the highest average Dice

Table 1. Development environments and requirements. (mandatory table)

System	Ubuntu 18.04.5
CPU	e Intel(R) Core(TM) i9-7900X CPU@3.30 GHz
RAM	32 × 4 GB; 2.67MT/s
GPU (number and type)	Four NVIDIA GeForce RTX 3090
CUDA version	12.5
Programming language	e.g., Python 3.10
Deep learning framework	torch 2.3.1, torchvision 0.18.1

score on foreground classes in the validation set, with evaluations performed after each epoch and the best checkpoint automatically saved.

Table 2. Training protocols.

Pre-trained Model	
Batch size	2
Patch size	176 × 112 × 112
Total epochs	1000
Optimizer	SGD
Initial learning rate (lr)	0.01
Lr decay schedule	0.9
Training time	18 h
Loss function	Dice and CE loss
Number of model parameters	31M
Number of flops	60G

4 Results and Discussion

The quantitative evaluation results on the AortaSeg24 training dataset are shown in Table 3. The proposed method demonstrates robust performance in anatomical regions with relatively consistent shape and clear boundaries across subjects. Specifically, regions such as Zone 5 (Avg. DSC: 0.876, NSD: 0.899), Zone 9 (DSC: 0.876, NSD: 0.859), and the Left and Right Common Iliac Arteries (DSC: 0.801 and 0.796, NSD: 0.891 and 0.853) achieve high segmentation accuracy. These regions benefit from strong appearance priors and high contrast in CT angiography, making them easier for the model to learn and delineate. However, the proposed method fails on small and tortuous vessels such as the Left Renal Artery and Zone 1. The failed cases are primarily attributed to a combination of anatomical complexity, low image contrast, and limited representation during training (Table 2).

Table 3. Quantitative evaluation results for the training dataset.

Anatomical Region	Avg. DSC	Avg. NSD
Zone 0	0.856 ± 0.110	0.72 ± 0.142
Innominate	0.778 ± 0.094	0.752 ± 0.17
Zone 1	0.621 ± 0.175	0.585 ± 0.127
Left Common Carotid	0.659 ± 0.186	0.893 ± 0.119
Zone 2	0.701 ± 0.152	0.567 ± 0.129
Left Subclavian Artery	0.760 ± 0.111	0.838 ± 0.091
Zone 3	0.754 ± 0.083	0.623 ± 0.078
Zone 4	0.787 ± 0.111	0.671 ± 0.117
Zone 5	0.876 ± 0.047	0.899 ± 0.067
Zone 6	0.718 ± 0.161	0.638 ± 0.175
Celiac Artery	0.658 ± 0.105	0.821 ± 0.142
Zone 7	0.671 ± 0.184	0.653 ± 0.114
SMA	0.645 ± 0.130	0.817 ± 0.183
Zone 8	0.697 ± 0.144	0.673 ± 0.155
Right Renal Artery	0.690 ± 0.090	0.895 ± 0.062
Left Renal Artery	0.561 ± 0.312	0.812 ± 0.148
Zone 9	0.876 ± 0.050	0.859 ± 0.132
Right Common Iliac Artery	0.796 ± 0.107	0.853 ± 0.074
Left Common Iliac Artery	0.801 ± 0.109	0.891 ± 0.13
Right Internal Iliac Artery	0.748 ± 0.107	0.811 ± 0.109
Left Internal Iliac Artery	0.671 ± 0.131	0.802 ± 0.111
Right External Iliac Artery	0.669 ± 0.131	0.778 ± 0.205
Left External Iliac Artery	0.649 ± 0.089	0.737 ± 0.171
Overall	**0.720 ± 0.084**	**0.765 ± 0.102**

4.1   Qualitative Results on Validation Set

We present one successful segmentation case and one failed case in Fig. 3, respectively. In the failed example, the segmentation model incorrectly labeled part of the Right External Iliac Artery as the Left External Iliac Artery, as highlighted by the red bounding box. This misclassification is likely due to the use of a simple cross-entropy loss function for zone classification, which may be insufficient for distinguishing anatomically adjacent or similar regions. Incorporating stronger anatomical priors or spatial constraints could help mitigate such errors and improve the consistency of predictions.

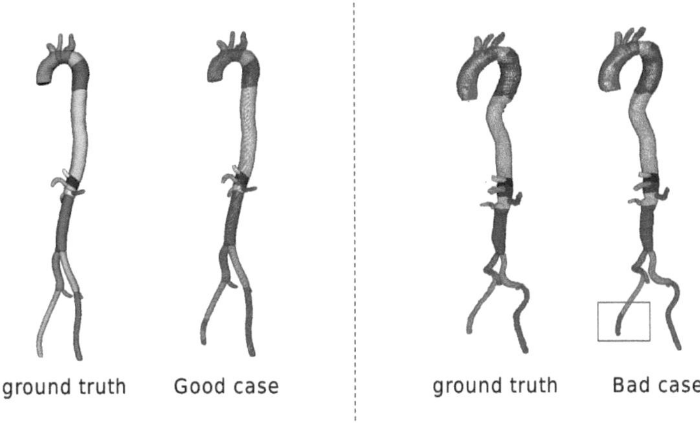

Fig. 3. Representative examples of good segmentation (left) and bad cases (right), highlighting the strengths and limitations of the proposed method. The DSC of Right External Iliac Atery of left and right cases are 0.687 and 0.523.

4.2   Results on Final Testing Set

Table 4 presents the quantitative evaluation results of our method on the AortaSeg24 testing dataset, comparing our method with the baseline CIS-UNet [3]. The performance is reported as the average Dice Similarity Coefficient (DSC) and Normalized Surface Dice (NSD) across 40 test cases for each anatomical region.

Overall, our method achieves a slightly higher average DSC of 0.729 ± 0.043 and NSD of 0.751 ± 0.047, compared to the baseline's 0.723 ± 0.058 and 0.746 ± 0.067, indicating competitive or improved performance. Notably, our method outperforms the baseline in several anatomically challenging regions, such as the Left and Right Renal Arteries (DSC: 0.686 and 0.723; NSD: 0.838 and 0.875), and the Left and Right Internal Iliac Arteries (DSC: 0.685 and 0.748; NSD: 0.806 and 0.869), suggesting better generalization in vessels with high inter-subject variability.

Moreover, substantial improvement is observed in the segmentation of the Left Common Carotid Artery (DSC: 0.779 vs. 0.743), where our model benefits from enhanced anatomical context modeling and refined boundary localization. On the other hand, a drop in performance is observed in the segmentation of the External Iliac Arteries, where the baseline model achieves higher accuracy. This may be attributed to occasional mislabeling in laterally symmetric structures, a known limitation in weakly-constrained classification schemes.

In summary, the proposed method delivers overall superior or comparable segmentation performance relative to CIS-UNet, particularly in regions with complex geometry or limited training representation. Future work may focus on incorporating stronger anatomical priors or multi-view consistency constraints to further reduce errors in symmetric or adjacent vessels.

Table 4. Quantitative evaluation on the AortaSeg24 testing dataset. The table reports average Dice and NSD scores (mean ± standard deviation) across all 40 test cases for each anatomical region. Authors may expand this table to include ablation studies or additional baselines.(mandatory table)

Anatomical Region	Our Method		Baseline Method [3]	
	Avg. DSC	Avg. NSD	Avg. DSC	Avg. NSD
Zone 0	0.875 ± 0.063	0.76 ± 0.142	0.880 ± 0.064	0.773 ± 0.119
Innominate	0.693 ± 0.161	0.745 ± 0.17	0.691 ± 0.164	0.739 ± 0.175
Zone 1	0.615 ± 0.169	0.551 ± 0.157	0.604 ± 0.164	0.560 ± 0.150
Left Common Carotid	0.779 ± 0.094	0.874 ± 0.099	0.743 ± 0.108	0.837 ± 0.117
Zone 2	0.665 ± 0.145	0.544 ± 0.139	0.659 ± 0.143	0.543 ± 0.153
Left Subclavian Artery	0.801 ± 0.075	0.866 ± 0.092	0.789 ± 0.115	0.859 ± 0.115
Zone 3	0.667 ± 0.165	0.533 ± 0.158	0.660 ± 0.171	0.517 ± 0.181
Zone 4	0.743 ± 0.133	0.638 ± 0.151	0.746 ± 0.122	0.620 ± 0.139
Zone 5	0.873 ± 0.061	0.829 ± 0.096	0.879 ± 0.054	0.826 ± 0.096
Zone 6	0.681 ± 0.159	0.625 ± 0.205	0.731 ± 0.123	0.678 ± 0.164
Celiac Artery	0.578 ± 0.19	0.729 ± 0.177	0.568 ± 0.178	0.728 ± 0.168
Zone 7	0.676 ± 0.14	0.644 ± 0.154	0.699 ± 0.116	0.660 ± 0.146
SMA	0.712 ± 0.121	0.807 ± 0.127	0.678 ± 0.131	0.782 ± 0.135
Zone 8	0.688 ± 0.131	0.661 ± 0.145	0.664 ± 0.160	0.656 ± 0.160
Right Renal Artery	0.723 ± 0.133	0.875 ± 0.142	0.697 ± 0.142	0.851 ± 0.140
Left Renal Artery	0.686 ± 0.164	0.838 ± 0.157	0.593 ± 0.199	0.742 ± 0.216
Zone 9	0.905 ± 0.048	0.893 ± 0.097	0.879 ± 0.081	0.860 ± 0.130
Right Common Iliac Artery	0.832 ± 0.113	0.873 ± 0.127	0.800 ± 0.132	0.840 ± 0.148
Left Common Iliac Artery	0.832 ± 0.089	0.886 ± 0.11	0.786 ± 0.135	0.842 ± 0.164
Right Internal Iliac Artery	0.748 ± 0.107	0.869 ± 0.103	0.661 ± 0.167	0.773 ± 0.179
Left Internal Iliac Artery	0.685 ± 0.163	0.806 ± 0.163	0.640 ± 0.197	0.767 ± 0.205
Right External Iliac Artery	0.646 ± 0.211	0.708 ± 0.217	0.789 ± 0.134	0.846 ± 0.143
Left External Iliac Artery	0.652 ± 0.161	0.716 ± 0.161	0.783 ± 0.151	0.851 ± 0.160
Overall	**0.729 ± 0.043**	**0.751 ± 0.047**	**0.723 ± 0.058**	**0.746 ± 0.067**

4.3   Limitation and Future Work

Despite the promising results achieved by our method, several limitations remain. First, the segmentation performance in anatomically symmetric or adjacent regions—such as the left and right external iliac arteries—was occasionally affected by misclassification. This issue likely arises from the use of a simple classification loss without incorporating explicit anatomical priors or spatial constraints, which makes it difficult to disambiguate regions with highly similar morphology and intensity patterns. Second, certain small or tortuous vessels exhibited high inter-subject variability and low contrast in CTA images, resulting in inconsistent boundary delineation across cases. These challenges highlight the need for more advanced strategies, such as the integration of shape-aware or topology-preserving losses, as well as multi-scale feature aggregation to better capture fine vascular structures. Moreover, our study was conducted on the AortaSeg24 challenge dataset, which, although diverse, may not fully represent the heterogeneity of real-world clinical populations. Future work should therefore investigate the generalizability of the proposed approach to multi-center datasets, explore domain adaptation techniques for handling scanner or protocol variability, and evaluate the clinical utility of the segmentation outputs in downstream applications such as treatment planning or surgical navigation.

In future work, we plan to incorporate anatomical priors or spatial attention mechanisms to guide the model toward more anatomically plausible predictions. Additionally, leveraging transformer-based architectures or multi-task learning strategies may help the model better capture long-range dependencies and structural context. Finally, extending the framework to support temporal consistency in longitudinal studies or generalization across multi-center datasets remains an important direction for clinical translation.

5   Conclusion

In this work, we proposed a robust segmentation framework for multi-class aortic anatomy in CTA images, achieving competitive performance on the AortaSeg24 dataset. Through careful architectural design and training strategies, our method demonstrates strong generalization across diverse anatomical regions, outperforming the baseline in several clinically relevant vessels. Quantitative results on the test set highlight the effectiveness of our approach in handling complex vascular structures. Future extensions will focus on enhancing anatomical consistency and further improving performance in challenging regions through the integration of prior knowledge and advanced modeling techniques.

Acknowledgments. We thank all data contributors for making the medical images publicly available, and GrandChallenge for providing the challenge platform. This study was conducted as part of the MICCAI 2024 AortaSeg24 Challenge.

Disclosure of Interests. The authors have no competing interests to declare that are relevant to the content of this article.

Ethical Compliance Statement. All data used was publicly available and anonymized.

References

1. Cao, H., et al.: Swin-Unet: Unet-like pure transformer for medical image segmentation. In: Karlinsky, L., Michaeli, T., Nishino, K. (eds.) ECCV 2022. LNCS, vol. 13803, pp. 205–218. Springer, Cham (2022). https://doi.org/10.1007/978-3-031-25066-8_9
2. Huang, H., et al.: UNet 3+: a full-scale connected UNet for medical image segmentation. In: ICASSP 2020-2020 IEEE International Conference on Acoustics, Speech and Signal Processing (ICASSP), pp. 1055–1059. IEEE (2020)

3. Imran, M., et al.: CIS-UNet: multi-class segmentation of the aorta in computed tomography angiography via context-aware shifted window self-attention. Comput. Med. Imaging Graph. **118**, 102470 (2024)

4. Imran, M., et al.: Multi-class segmentation of aortic branches and zones in computed tomography angiography: the aortaseg24 challenge. arXiv preprint arXiv:2502.05330 (2025)

5. Isensee, F., et al.: nnU-net revisited: a call for rigorous validation in 3D medical image segmentation. In: Linguraru, M.G., et al. (eds.) MICCAI 2024. LNCS, vol. 15009, pp. 488–498. Springer, Cham (2024). https://doi.org/10.1007/978-3-031-72114-4_47

6. Krebs, J.R., et al.: Volumetric analysis of acute uncomplicated type b aortic dissection using an automated deep learning aortic zone segmentation model. J. Vasc. Surg. **80**(4), 1025–1034 (2024)

7. Labropoulos, N., et al.: Study of the venous reflux progression. J. Vasc. Surg. **41**(2), 291–295 (2005)

8. Li, X., Chen, H., Qi, X., Dou, Q., Fu, C.W., Heng, P.A.: H-DenseUNet: hybrid densely connected UNet for liver and tumor segmentation from CT volumes. IEEE Trans. Med. Imaging **37**(12), 2663–2674 (2018)

9. Paulauskaite-Taraseviciene, A., Siaulys, J., Jankauskas, A., Jakuskaite, G.: A robust blood vessel segmentation technique for angiographic images employing multi-scale filtering approach. J. Clin. Med. **14**(2), 354 (2025)

10. Radl, L., et al.: AVT: multicenter aortic vessel tree CTA dataset collection with ground truth segmentation masks. Data Brief **40**, 107801 (2022)

A Mamba-Based Method with Gated Attention for Human Aorta Segmentation

Jinghua Yue[1], Fugen Zhou[1], and Bo Liu[1,2]

[1] Image Processing Center, Beihang University, Beijing, China
[2] State Key Laboratory of High-Efficiency Reusable Aerospace Transportation Technology, Beijing 102206, China
bo.liu@buaa.edu.cn

Abstract. We propose a segmentation framework for multi-class aortic segmentation that combines global context modeling using a Mamba-based module as the core component, with an additional gated attention mechanism explored for spatially adaptive feature refinement. To enhance anatomical plausibility, we incorporate a post-processing step based on anatomical location constraints. On the AortaSeg24 test set, our method achieved an average Dice score of 0.675 and NSD of 0.693. While the overall scores appear lower than the baseline, further analysis revealed that the near-zero scores for the last two anatomical classes were caused by a submission error. Excluding these, our model attained a Dice of 0.738 and NSD of 0.758, outperforming the baseline. Qualitative evaluation highlights strengths in major vessel segmentation but shows occasional boundary ambiguity in multi-segment regions and inconsistent predictions at distal vessel ends. These issues are likely due to limited patch-level context and the absence of clinical priors guiding the extent of vessel annotations. Future improvements will focus on context-aware modeling and clinical knowledge integration to enhance robustness and accuracy.

Keywords: Aorta segmentation · Mamba · Gated attention

1 Introduction

Diseases involving the aorta and its major branches, such as aneurysms, dissections, and congenital malformations, are among the most life-threatening cardiovascular conditions. Timely and accurate assessment through medical imaging is essential for diagnosis, surgical planning, and postoperative monitoring. In particular, the precise delineation of the aorta and its branching structures from imaging data plays a critical role in guiding clinical decisions and improving patient outcomes [1]. However, automatic segmentation of the aorta remains a formidable challenge due to its intricate anatomical morphology, complex branching topology, and often indistinct boundaries between vascular structures and surrounding tissues. These factors are further compounded by

M. Imran et al. (Eds.): AortaSeg 2024, LNCS 16399, pp. 109–121, 2026.
https://doi.org/10.1007/978-3-032-14246-7_10

inter-patient variability, imaging artifacts, and low contrast between adjacent anatomical regions. As a result, conventional segmentation algorithms frequently fail to achieve satisfactory accuracy and generalizability in this context.

In recent years, deep learning-based methods, particularly convolutional neural networks (CNNs), have demonstrated remarkable success across a wide range of medical image segmentation tasks, including vascular structures [11]. CNNs are highly effective at extracting local patterns and spatial features. T. Lyu et al. [12] proposed a two-step method using 3D and 2D CNNs with edge enhancement to segment dissected aorta. Xiang D et al. [17] designed a flap attention module to segment aortic dissection. However, their inherent limitation in modeling long-range dependencies restricts their ability to fully capture the global anatomical context of complex vascular systems like the aorta and its branches. This often leads to errors in distinguishing between similar-looking branches or in maintaining the continuity of elongated structures. To address the limitations of local receptive fields in CNNs, Vision Transformers (ViTs) [2] introduced pure self-attention mechanisms for image representation learning. ViTs excel at modeling long-range interactions, offering a potential solution for capturing complex spatial dependencies [14]. The ZOZI-seg model [9] segments each aortic compartmentusing a two-stage architecture that combines a 3D Transformer for global context and a 3D UNet for local texture refinement. Nevertheless, the computational burden of self-attention in Transformer, which scales quadratically with input size, becomes prohibitive when applied to high-resolution volumetric medical images. Furthermore, while current approaches typically address global aorta segmentation or coarse subdivision, there is a lack of methods tailored for detailed, clinically guided partitioning of aortic subregions. Such fine-grained segmentation poses greater challenges for network design and requires enhanced representational capability.

Recently, State Space Models (SSMs) [5], particularly the Structured State Space sequence model (S4) [4], have emerged as an efficient alternative for sequence modeling, offering linear time and space complexity. Building on this foundation, the Mamba model [3] integrates selective input mechanisms with hardware-aware optimizations, providing a highly efficient and scalable architecture for capturing long-range dependencies in dense input domains. By blending SSM blocks with simple linear layers, Mamba achieves state-of-the-art performance in long-sequence modeling tasks, while significantly reducing computational cost during both training and inference.

Motivated by these developments, we propose a novel aortic segmentation framework that integrates the strengths of CNNs and Mamba-based long-range modeling. Specifically, we incorporate convolutional modules to capture fine-grained local features and fuse them with Mamba blocks in the encoder to effectively learn global contextual representations. In addition, we investigate a gated attention module to mitigate the semantic gap introduced by skip connections and to adaptively refine the information transmitted between encoder and decoder. Furthermore, certain small aortic branches exhibit symmetric structures, which can lead to confusion during segmentation due to their visual similarity. To address this, we incorporate a simple post-processing step based on spatial positional relationships to correct such misclassifications, thereby improving the anatomical plausibility of the final segmentation.

2   Method

2.1   Network Overview

To address the challenge of segmenting multiple regions of the aorta, we developed a network architecture that integrates the Mamba model. Figure 1 illustrates the overall structure of the proposed method. Due to its symmetrical encoder-decoder architecture and robust performance, U-Net [15] has become a benchmark in medical image segmentation tasks. Therefore, we adopted U-Net as the backbone network for our approach. However, the intricate structure of the aorta poses challenges for traditional U-Net architectures. To overcome this, we integrated the local feature extraction capabilities of convolutional modules with the long-range dependency capture offered by the Mamba model in the encoder phase, effectively handling the complex morphology of the aorta. Moreover, we explored the use of a gated attention module to alleviate the semantic gap between encoder and decoder features [16].

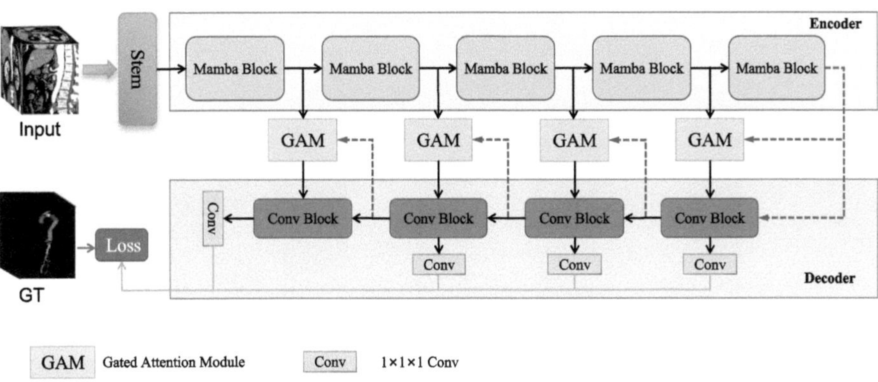

Fig. 1. The network architecture.

2.2   Backbone Network

Given the effectiveness and stability of U-Net in medical image segmentation, our method adopts U-Net as the backbone network. To enhance vascular feature extraction, the standard convolutional modules in the encoder are replaced with residual convolutional blocks, improving feature propagation and information retention. The backbone consists of a stem module, five encoder blocks, and four decoder blocks. The encoder employs a convolution with a stride of 2 for downsampling, while the decoder performs upsampling to restore the original image resolution.

2.3 Mamba: Selective Structured State Space Sequence Models with a Scan

Recent studies have increasingly incorporated the Mamba model into image processing tasks. To address the complex structure of aortic vessels, we leverage the linear scaling capability of the Mamba model to enhance the CNN's ability to capture long-range dependencies, as illustrated in Fig. 2(a). Inspired by the encoder design of U-Mamba [13], we adopt a similar structure to enhance feature representation. Each encoder block is composed of two consecutive residual blocks, followed by instance normalization and Leaky ReLU activation.

The image features, initially shaped as (B, C, H, W, D), are first flattened and transposed to (B, L, C), where L denotes the product of H, W, and D. After layer normalization, the features are passed into the Mamba block, which contains two parallel branches. In the first branch, the features are expanded to (B, 2L, C) via a linear layer, followed by a 1D convolution, activation by the SiLU function, and processing through a structured state space model (SSM) layer. The second branch follows a similar process: feature expansion to (B, 2L, C), a linear transformation, and SiLU activation. The outputs from both branches are then combined using the Hadamard product. Finally, the combined features are projected back to the original dimension (B, L, C), reshaped, and transposed to (B, C, H, W, D).

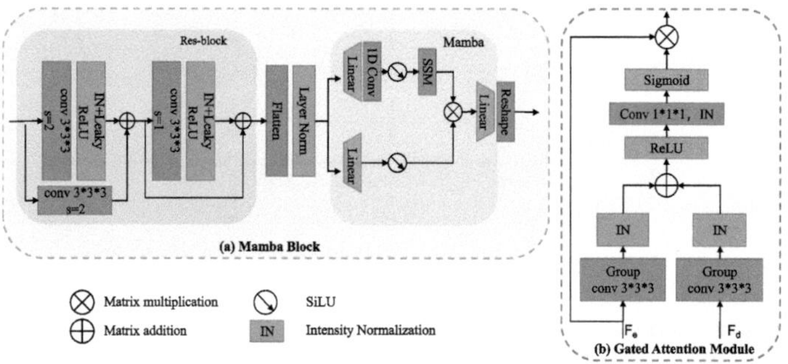

Fig. 2. The detailed structure of the block of the encoder with Mamba and the gated attention module.

2.4 The Gated Attention Module

To bridge the semantic discrepancy between encoder and decoder features caused by conventional skip connections, we incorporate a gated attention module designed to refine feature transmission in a task-aware manner. Rather than serving as a dominant component, this module plays a complementary role by guiding the network to focus on vascular regions while reducing distractions from surrounding tissues and visually confounding vessel classes. This is helpful in our task where anatomical continuity and inter-class distinction are challenging due to similar morphology among subtypes. As shown in Fig. 2(b), the module receives feature maps from both the encoder and the corresponding decoder level. These are independently processed by 3×3 group convolutions to extract local vascular patterns with efficiency. After normalization through instance normalization, the two feature streams are combined via element-wise addition, followed by a ReLU activation to enhance non-linearity. A 1×1 convolution and another normalization step are then applied to derive a single-channel attention map, which is passed through a Sigmoid function to obtain spatially adaptive weights. These weights are subsequently used to recalibrate the encoder features, providing modest yet consistent improvements in supporting the decoder for fine-grained vascular segmentation.

2.5 Anatomy-Aware Post-processing

In clinical cases involving highly symmetric vascular branches, we observed that the segmentation model occasionally misassigns labels between bilateral structures, especially the left and right external iliac arteries (see the purple and pink segments in Fig. 3(a) with yellow arrows indicating the confusion). We suspect that sliding-window inference contributes significantly to this issue by introducing local ambiguity that affects spatial consistency. To mitigate this issue, we introduce a lightweight post-processing refinement module that adjusts misaligned predictions based on anatomical symmetry and spatial positioning.

Specifically, as illustrated in Algorithm 1, the post-processing procedure first extracts all connected components labeled as external iliac arteries. It then identifies the reference region (right common iliac artery) and filters components located inferior to it. For each of these components, the minimum x-coordinate is compared against that of the reference to determine whether it belongs to the left or right side, and the label is reassigned accordingly. This correction leverages the spatial symmetry of bilateral vascular structures to mitigate local prediction inconsistencies. The left-right assignment is based on the spatial convention that the voxel x-coordinate increases from the patient's right to left in

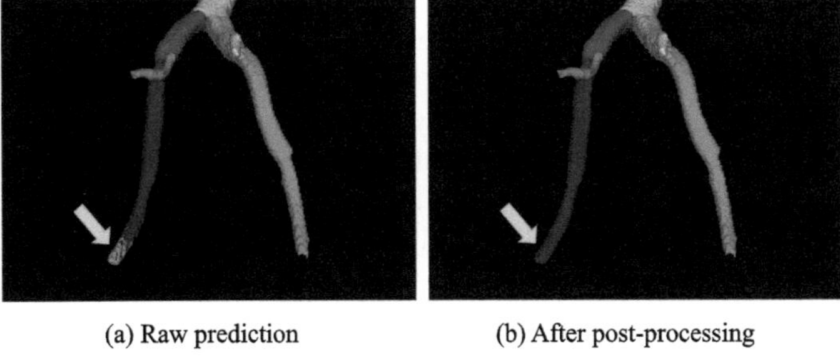

(a) Raw prediction   (b) After post-processing

Fig. 3. Correction of label confusion in symmetric vascular structures.

axial CT images. As shown in Fig. 3(b), this post-processing step successfully eliminates the label confusion.

Algorithm 1: Anatomy-Aware Post-processing

Input: Segmentation mask $\mathbf{M}$, ℓ_{left} (left iliac), ℓ_{right} (right iliac), ℓ_{ref} (Right Common Iliac)

Output: Corrected mask $\mathbf{M}'$

begin
    $\mathbf{M}' \leftarrow \mathbf{M}$
    $\mathbf{B} \leftarrow (\mathbf{M} = \ell_{left}) \vee (\mathbf{M} = \ell_{right})$
    $\mathcal{R} \leftarrow \text{COORDINATES}(\mathbf{M} = \ell_{ref})$
    $z_{max} \leftarrow \max(\mathcal{R}^z)$, $x_{min} \leftarrow \min(\mathcal{R}^x)$
    $(\mathbf{L}, N) \leftarrow \text{CONNECTEDCOMPONENTS}(\mathbf{B})$
    for $i \leftarrow 1$ **to** N **do**
        $\mathcal{C} \leftarrow \text{COORDINATES}(\mathbf{L} = i)$
        $z_{min} \leftarrow \min(\mathcal{C}^z)$
        if $z_{min} \leq z_{max}$ **then**
            $x_{min}^{(i)} \leftarrow \min(\mathcal{C}^x)$
            if $x_{min}^{(i)} < x_{min}$ **then**
                $\mathbf{M}'[\mathbf{L} = i] \leftarrow \ell_{right}$
            else
                $\mathbf{M}'[\mathbf{L} = i] \leftarrow \ell_{left}$
            end
        end
    end
    return $\mathbf{M}'$
end

---

3 Experiments

3.1 Dataset and Evaluation Protocol

The dataset used in this study is provided by the AortaSeg24 Challenge [7,10], organized as part of MICCAI 2024. The challenge focuses on multi-class segmentation of the aorta in computed tomography angiography (CTA), including 23 clinically relevant aortic branches and zones. The dataset consists of 100 annotated 3D CTA scans from patients with uncomplicated type B aortic dissection. Each volume was manually annotated by trained researchers and reviewed by an experienced vascular surgeon to ensure clinical accuracy. The annotations include major aortic branches (e.g., renal, iliac, and celiac arteries) and SVS/STS zones, following standard clinical guidelines. All volumes were resampled to an isotropic resolution of $1 \times 1 \times 1$ mm^3 for consistency. Of the 100 scans, 50 were provided for training. The remaining 50 were split between validation and hidden test sets by the organizers.

To quantitatively assess the performance of our multi-class aortic segmentation model, in the training dataset, we report the average Dice, Recall, Jaccard

Index, and Normalized Surface Distance (NSD) across all anatomical classes. These metrics were selected to provide a balanced evaluation of both region-level overlap (Dice, Recall, Jaccard) and boundary-level accuracy (NSD). In the final test phase, we followed the official evaluation metrics of the challenge and reported the average Dice and Normalized Surface Distance within a 2 mm tolerance.

3.2 Implementation Details

We adopted the publicly available nnU-Net v2 framework [8] for both training and evaluation, employing its default data pre-processing and post-processing strategies. Model optimization was performed using stochastic gradient descent (SGD) with Nesterov momentum, starting from an initial learning rate of $1e-2$. Training was conducted with a batch size of 2 and 250 iterations per epoch. Considering both convergence requirements and computational efficiency, we set the maximum number of epochs to 500, which is a reduction from the nnU-Net default of 1000 epochs, while still ensuring stable convergence across all experimental models. All experiments were conducted on a single NVIDIA A100 GPU to ensure consistent computational conditions. More detailed information is shown in the Table 1 and Table 2.

Table 1. Development environments and requirements.

System	Ubuntu 22.04.1
CPU	Intel(R) Xeon(R) Silver 4310 CPU @ 2.10 GHz
RAM	2×64 GB; 2666MT/s
GPU (number and type)	One NVIDIA A100 40G
CUDA version	12.4
Programming language	Python 3.10.14
Deep learning framework	torch 2.0.1, torchvision 0.15.2

4   Results and Discussion

In this section, we comprehensively evaluate the proposed method through quantitative comparisons, qualitative visualizations, and challenge test results. First, we conduct ablation studies on the 50 public training cases to demonstrate the effectiveness of our model design. Then, we present visual segmentation results, highlighting both successful and challenging cases, and discuss relevant observations. Finally, we report the model's performance on the challenge test dataset, analyze the underlying cause of an unexpected degradation in specific categories, and provide a detailed explanation based on the validation results in the model development phase to ensure transparency and fairness.

Table 2. Training protocols.

Pre-trained Model	
Batch size	2
Patch size	$176 \times 112 \times 112$
Total epochs	500
Optimizer	SGD with Nesterov momentum
Initial learning rate (lr)	0.01
Lr decay schedule	Poly LR decay with power 0.9
Training time	32 h
Loss function	Dice and Cross Entropy
Number of model parameters	6.90M[a]
Number of flops	6902.69G[b]

[a] https://github.com/sksq96/pytorch-summary
[b] https://github.com/facebookresearch/fvcore

4.1 Evaluation Results for the Training Dataset

To ensure the fairness and reproducibility of all experiments, we consistently adopt a fixed split of 40 cases for training and 10 cases for test across all evaluations.

To validate the effectiveness of each proposed component, we conducted a detailed ablation study as shown in Table 3. Compared with the baseline (Row 1), incorporating the Mamba module in the encoder (Row 2) significantly improves the model's ability to capture structural boundaries, increasing the Dice score from 0.732 to 0.744, and NSD from 0.774 to 0.780. These results demonstrate the benefit of long-range global modeling. The GAM alone (Row 3) does not improve performance. When combined with Mamba (Row 4 and Row 5), it helps the model achieve the best results, suggesting that GAM can complement Mamba but is not effective by itself. The final post-processing step further boosts performance by enforcing anatomical consistency and correcting local ambiguities. More detailed results for each category are shown in the Table 4.

Table 3. Ablation study of the proposed modules.

Method	Dice ↑	Recall ↑	Jaccard ↑	NSD ↑
Baseline	0.732 ± 0.028	0.756 ± 0.041	0.597 ± 0.026	0.774 ± 0.023
+Mamba	0.744 ± 0.023	0.774 ± 0.044	0.610 ± 0.024	0.780± 0.031
+GAM	0.730 ± 0.033	0.762 ± 0.042	0.595 ± 0.033	0.761 ± 0.030
Ours w/o post	0.747 ± 0.022	0.778 ± 0.041	0.613 ± 0.023	0.779 ± 0.022
Ours	0.752 ± 0.023	0.784 ± 0.039	0.621 ± 0.025	0.787 ± 0.026

Table 4. Quantitative evaluation results for the training dataset in 23 classes.

Anatomical Region	Avg. DSC	Avg. NSD
Zone 0	0.899 ± 0.032	0.824 ± 0.058
Innominate	0.774 ± 0.144	0.836 ± 0.131
Zone 1	0.613 ± 0.194	0.614 ± 0.148
Left Common Carotid	0.737 ± 0.125	0.829 ± 0.114
Zone 2	0.685 ± 0.094	0.592 ± 0.113
Left Subclavian Artery	0.746 ± 0.121	0.820 ± 0.139
Zone 3	0.664 ± 0.120	0.518 ± 0.168
Zone 4	0.713 ± 0.111	0.585 ± 0.130
Zone 5	0.866 ± 0.050	0.786 ± 0.075
Zone 6	0.709 ± 0.090	0.621 ± 0.122
Celiac Artery	0.658 ± 0.156	0.795 ± 0.137
Zone 7	0.689 ± 0.110	0.713 ± 0.128
SMA	0.694 ± 0.122	0.797 ± 0.134
Zone 8	0.671 ± 0.176	0.686 ± 0.193
Right Renal Artery	0.668 ± 0.236	0.830 ± 0.213
Left Renal Artery	0.724 ± 0.081	0.869 ± 0.100
Zone 9	0.891 ± 0.033	0.891 ± 0.071
Right Common Iliac Artery	0.835 ± 0.126	0.900 ± 0.141
Left Common Iliac Artery	0.877 ± 0.047	0.931 ± 0.067
Right Internal Iliac Artery	0.778 ± 0.047	0.918 ± 0.064
Left Internal Iliac Artery	0.761 ± 0.092	0.879 ± 0.104
Right External Iliac Artery w/o post	0.802 ± 0.069	0.845 ± 0.085
Left External Iliac Artery w/o post	0.850 ± 0.045	0.0899 ± 0.057
Right External Iliac Artery	0.741 ± 0.086	0.918 ± 0.055
Left External Iliac Artery	0.786 ± 0.070	0.958 ± 0.044
Overall w/o post	**0.747 ± 0.022**	**0.779 ± 0.022**
Overall	**0.752 ± 0.024**	**0.787 ± 0.026**

4.2 Qualitative Results on Training Dataset

To further analyze the model's segmentation behavior, we present two representative cases from the training dataset: the best-performing case (Case 49) and the worst-performing case (Case 24), which achieved Dice scores of 0.791 and 0.721, respectively. As illustrated in the Fig. 4, the regions with notable segmentation errors are highlighted using yellow arrows for clarity.

In the worst-performing case, segmentation errors were primarily observed in multi-segment vascular structures, where boundary ambiguity led to misclassification across adjacent zones. For instance, portions of Zone 4 were erroneously assigned to Zone 5. Additionally, discrepancies were identified at the distal ends of branching vessels, where the predicted masks either over-extended beyond the anatomical region or failed to capture the entire segment.

These issues may stem from several factors. First, the fixed patch size used during training might have limited the model's ability to capture sufficient contextual information, especially for long-range dependencies in extended vascular structures. Second, the absence of clinical priors could have contributed to the ambiguity in anatomical delineation, particularly in zones where the boundary definition is not strictly anatomical but also informed by procedural relevance.

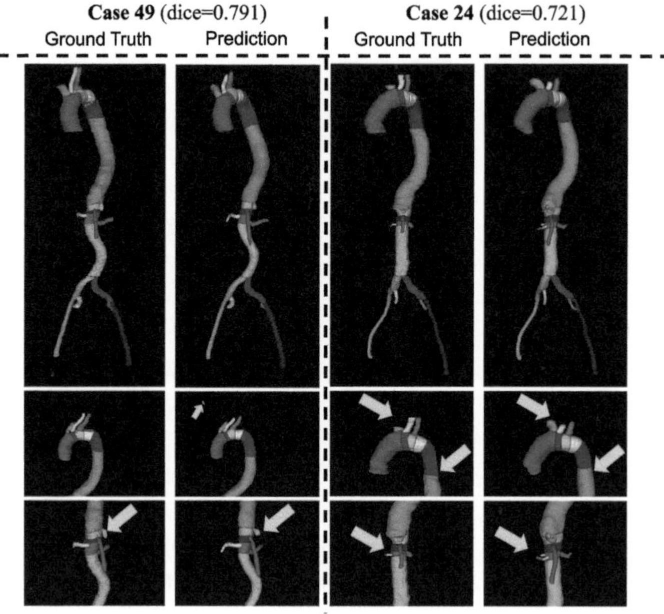

Fig. 4. The qualitative results with the best-performing case (case 49) and the worst-performing case (case 24).

4.3   Results on Final Testing Set

Table 5 presents a quantitative comparison based on official results between our method and the official baseline model (CIS-UNet [6]) on the final testing set. In this stage, our model was trained using all 50 training data sets. Our model achieved an average Dice score of 0.675 and an average Normalized Surface Distance (NSD) of 0.693, whereas the baseline model attained 0.723 and 0.746, respectively. While the overall performance appears lower, further inspection revealed that the segmentation scores for the last two anatomical structures were close to zero. Upon review, we identified that this drop was caused by an unintended error during the final submission phase, where incorrect label names were introduced in the post-processing stage. This issue was due to a submission oversight on our part. For reference, we include the result performance during the model development stage, where our method achieved a higher average Dice score compared to the baseline. All performance metrics on the final test stage and the model development stage were directly provided by the official AortaSeg24 organizers.

To further highlight the performance gain of our method over the baseline, we additionally report the average scores over the first 21 anatomical categories, which are unaffected by the aforementioned issue. In this restricted evaluation, our approach achieved a Dice score of 0.738 and an NSD of 0.758, outperforming the baseline scores of 0.717 and 0.736, respectively. The performance improvement is also consistently reflected across multiple individual anatomical categories, further demonstrating the effectiveness and robustness of our proposed method.

Table 5. Quantitative evaluation on the AortaSeg24 testing dataset and validation dataset (at model development phase) using official metrics. The table reports average Dice and NSD scores (mean ± standard deviation) across all 40 test cases and average Dice scores across all 10 validation cases for each anatomical region.

Anatomical Region	Our Method		Baseline Method [6]		Our Method*	Baseline [6]*
	Avg. DSC	Avg. NSD	Avg. DSC	Avg. NSD	Avg. DSC	Avg. DSC
Zone 0	0.866 ± 0.111	0.758 ± 0.146	0.880 ± 0.064	0.773 ± 0.119	0.832 ± 0.116	0.850 ± 0.117
Innominate	0.763 ± 0.136	0.807 ± 0.139	0.691 ± 0.164	0.739 ± 0.175	0.787 ± 0.082	0.793 ± 0.066
Zone 1	0.617 ± 0.157	0.555 ± 0.159	0.604 ± 0.164	0.560 ± 0.150	0.644 ± 0.190	0.603 ± 0.171
Left Common Carotid	0.799 ± 0.074	0.898 ± 0.077	0.743 ± 0.108	0.837 ± 0.117	0.708 ± 0.114	0.644 ± 0.211
Zone 2	0.678 ± 0.127	0.561 ± 0.131	0.659 ± 0.143	0.543 ± 0.153	0.701 ± 0.161	0.695 ± 0.183
Left Subclavian Artery	0.812 ± 0.074	0.883 ± 0.089	0.789 ± 0.115	0.859 ± 0.115	0.782 ± 0.074	0.688 ± 0.254
Zone 3	0.692 ± 0.147	0.550 ± 0.161	0.660 ± 0.171	0.517 ± 0.181	0.760 ± 0.075	0.752 ± 0.065
Zone 4	0.784 ± 0.100	0.655 ± 0.135	0.746 ± 0.122	0.620 ± 0.139	0.787 ± 0.108	0.786 ± 0.104
Zone 5	0.890 ± 0.086	0.844 ± 0.116	0.879 ± 0.054	0.826 ± 0.096	0.866 ± 0.055	0.870 ± 0.055
Zone 6	0.632 ± 0.210	0.592 ± 0.217	0.731 ± 0.123	0.678 ± 0.164	0.627 ± 0.236	0.705 ± 0.122
Celiac Artery	0.604 ± 0.177	0.749 ± 0.186	0.568 ± 0.178	0.728 ± 0.168	0.615 ± 0.085	0.661 ± 0.119
Zone 7	0.646 ± 0.203	0.627 ± 0.192	0.699 ± 0.116	0.660 ± 0.146	0.621 ± 0.218	0.609 ± 0.186
SMA	0.695 ± 0.156	0.803 ± 0.166	0.678 ± 0.131	0.782 ± 0.135	0.569 ± 0.100	0.689 ± 0.133
Zone 8	0.681 ± 0.187	0.670 ± 0.183	0.664 ± 0.160	0.656 ± 0.160	0.708 ± 0.115	0.640 ± 0.162
Right Renal Artery	0.712 ± 0.165	0.864 ± 0.190	0.697 ± 0.142	0.851 ± 0.140	0.630 ± 0.084	0.592 ± 0.137
Left Renal Artery	0.658 ± 0.212	0.793 ± 0.230	0.593 ± 0.199	0.742 ± 0.216	0.580 ± 0.318	0.472 ± 0.271
Zone 9	0.883 ± 0.154	0.874 ± 0.171	0.879 ± 0.081	0.860 ± 0.130	0.887 ± 0.046	0.868 ± 0.059
Right Common Iliac Artery	0.819 ± 0.159	0.859 ± 0.168	0.800 ± 0.132	0.840 ± 0.148	0.806 ± 0.044	0.792 ± 0.089
Left Common Iliac Artery	0.821 ± 0.149	0.882 ± 0.170	0.786 ± 0.135	0.842 ± 0.164	0.817 ± 0.092	0.787 ± 0.103
Right Internal Iliac Artery	0.756 ± 0.104	0.876 ± 0.111	0.661 ± 0.167	0.773 ± 0.179	0.735 ± 0.103	0.670 ± 0.119
Left Internal Iliac Artery	0.697 ± 0.164	0.820 ± 0.181	0.640 ± 0.197	0.767 ± 0.205	0.708 ± 0.069	0.605 ± 0.165
Right External Iliac Artery	0.000 ± 0.000	0.000 ± 0.000	0.789 ± 0.134	0.846 ± 0.143	0.802 ± 0.071	0.748 ± 0.112
Left External Iliac Artery	0.025 ± 0.111	0.028 ± 0.121	0.783 ± 0.151	0.851 ± 0.160	0.755 ± 0.041	0.728 ± 0.083
Overall	**0.675 ± 0.072**	**0.693 ± 0.079**	**0.723 ± 0.058**	**0.746 ± 0.067**	**0.727 ± 0.045**	**0.706 ± 0.050**
Average (first 21 anatomical categories)	**0.738**	**0.758**	**0.717**	**0.736**	/	/

Note: * indicates validation results provided by the AortaSeg24 organizers during the model development phase.

5 Conclusion

In this work, we propose a simple yet effective segmentation framework for multi-class aortic structure delineation, primarily leveraging global dependency modeling through the Mamba module, with an optional gated attention module (GAM) for spatially adaptive feature refinement. Ablation studies indicate that the inclusion of long-range context modeling substantially improves both region-wise and boundary-level accuracy in complex vascular segmentation tasks, while the GAM only contributes when combined with Mamba. Our method also integrates an anatomy-aware post-processing module, which helps correct disconnected or misclassified regions based on spatial priors. Despite its effectiveness, our method has several limitations. The model occasionally missegments multi-branch structures by assigning overlapping areas to adjacent regions, and produces inconsistent predictions at vascular terminals, leading to over- or under-segmentation. These issues may stem from limited contextual information within small patches and the absence of clinical priors. Incorporating clinical priors may help improve alignment between predictions and clinically relevant structures.

Acknowledgements. This study was funded by Beijing Natural Science Foundation under Grant L232037, Grant L222034, and Grant L242112; in part by the National Natural Science Foundation of China under Grant 12375359.

Disclosure of Interests. The authors have no competing interests to declare that are relevant to the content of this article.

Ethical Compliance Statement. All data used was publicly available and anonymized.

References

1. Bednarska, M., Stolarz, E., Stopiński, M., Biederman, A., Polkowski, J., Kapuściński, O.: Early diagnosis of aortic dissection. The key to successful surgical treatment. Med. Sci. Monit. **2**(3), CS348–CS351 (1996)
2. Dosovitskiy, A.: An image is worth 16×16 words: transformers for image recognition at scale. arXiv preprint arXiv:2010.11929 (2020)
3. Gu, A., Dao, T.: Mamba: linear-time sequence modeling with selective state spaces. arXiv preprint arXiv:2312.00752 (2023)
4. Gu, A., Goel, K., Ré, C.: Efficiently modeling long sequences with structured state spaces. arXiv preprint arXiv:2111.00396 (2021)
5. Gu, A., et al.: Combining recurrent, convolutional, and continuous-time models with linear state space layers. Adv. Neural. Inf. Process. Syst. **34**, 572–585 (2021)
6. Imran, M., et al.: CIS-UNet: multi-class segmentation of the aorta in computed tomography angiography via context-aware shifted window self-attention. Comput. Med. Imaging Graph. **118**, 102470 (2024)
7. Imran, M., et al.: Multi-class segmentation of aortic branches and zones in computed tomography angiography: the aortaseg24 challenge. arXiv preprint arXiv:2502.05330 (2025)

8. Isensee, F., Jaeger, P.F., Kohl, S.A., Petersen, J., Maier-Hein, K.H.: nnU-net: a self-configuring method for deep learning-based biomedical image segmentation. Nat. Methods **18**(2), 203–211 (2021)

9. Jung, J.H., et al.: ZOZI-seg: a transformer and UNet cascade network with zoom-out and zoom-in scheme for aortic dissection segmentation in enhanced CT images. Comput. Biol. Med. **175**, 108494 (2024)

10. Krebs, J.R., et al.: Volumetric analysis of acute uncomplicated type b aortic dissection using an automated deep learning aortic zone segmentation model. J. Vasc. Surg. **80**(4), 1025–1034 (2024)

11. Litjens, G., et al.: A survey on deep learning in medical image analysis. Med. Image Anal. **42**, 60–88 (2017)

12. Lyu, T., et al.: Dissected aorta segmentation using convolutional neural networks. Comput. Methods Programs Biomed. **211**, 106417 (2021)

13. Ma, J., Li, F., Wang, B.: U-mamba: enhancing long-range dependency for biomedical image segmentation. arXiv preprint arXiv:2401.04722 (2024)

14. Pu, Q., Xi, Z., Yin, S., Zhao, Z., Zhao, L.: Advantages of transformer and its application for medical image segmentation: a survey. Biomed. Eng. Online **23**(1), 14 (2024)

15. Ronneberger, O., Fischer, P., Brox, T.: U-net: convolutional networks for biomedical image segmentation. In: Navab, N., Hornegger, J., Wells, W.M., Frangi, A.F. (eds.) MICCAI 2015, Part III. LNCS, vol. 9351, pp. 234–241. Springer, Cham (2015). https://doi.org/10.1007/978-3-319-24574-4_28

16. Wang, R., Lei, T., Cui, R., Zhang, B., Meng, H., Nandi, A.K.: Medical image segmentation using deep learning: a survey. IET Image Process. **16**(5), 1243–1267 (2022)

17. Xiang, D., et al.: ADSeg: a flap-attention-based deep learning approach for aortic dissection segmentation. Patterns **4**(5) (2023)

Author Index